ESSENTIAL ADVAITA

NONDUAL REALIZATION

SHIVADA
AMRITA

ESSENTIAL ADVAITA
NONDUAL REALIZATION

iUniverse books may be ordered through booksellers or by contacting:

iUniverse
1663 Liberty Drive
Bloomington, IN 47403
www.iuniverse.com
844-349-9409

ISBN: 978-1-6632-3572-5 (sc)
ISBN: 978-1-6632-3573-2 (e)

Library of Congress Control Number: 2022902680

Print information available on the last page.

iUniverse rev. date: 02/08/2022

CONTENTS

DEDICATION

This book is dedicated to my daughters Alysha Jyoti, Stefanie Robin, and Lindsey Scooter, whom I instructed in TM as children. Their unconditional love and support have been an immeasurable joy.

My deepest gratitude to his Holiness Maharishi Mahesh Yogi, an incredibly bright light of consciousness that provided the Transcendental Meditation Program, Science of Creative Intelligence, and Maharishi Vedic Science to the world. Jai Guru Dev.

FOREWORD

The sage Adi Shankara brought Advaita or Nonduality forward. It was a new framing of the ancient message of Vedanta, the end of the Veda or final knowledge.

In his brief life, Shankara converted many spiritual leaders through debate. He also wrote commentaries on key Vedic texts. And he founded four seats of learning in the cardinal directions of India. They have recorded the lineage of masters of those seats since.

Based on that lineage, he founded the first seat in the North at Jyotir Math in about 497 BC. This was well before western scholars generally placed his life.

As has happened throughout history, the core means of unfolding Nondual awareness is revived, then lost again within 3-400 years. Those techniques that bring regular Samadhi or what the Upanishads call Turiya, the fourth (a state besides waking, dreaming, and sleeping), are lost. Teachers become mind-based and come to recommend mental effort and control, the opposite of the required letting go.

The stages of enlightenment thus become rare, and Advaita degraded into intellectual arguments. Some came to confuse passing experiences of Oneness with lived Nonduality. Indeed, a taste can offer recognition of Nondual reality. But true Nonduality is lived in our very being. It isn't a concept in mind or a belief.

Some who reached Self-Realization dismissed the world as an illusion and declared awake consciousness within as Nondual.

However, dismissing part of your experience is not reality. Self Realization is a stage of dwaita or duality, a reality of singular inner consciousness and a separate outer world. This is an important stage for creating a platform for Nonduality. But that is not yet it.

More profoundly, the Self recognizes its reality also underlies the world's appearance. We recognize subject and object as one, and they unite in wholeness.

When consciousness comes to know itself fully, we can go beyond it and discover its source in Brahman. Even the subtle dualities of consciousness and not consciousness, existing and non-existing, collapse together into one totality. We find the world to be an uncreated appearance. And yet, it's one with purpose. Brahman is a collapsing of all paradoxes, although describing it is paradoxical.

Adi Shankara himself illustrated this with his famous verse:
"The world is unreal
Only Brahman is real
The world is Brahman"

In other words, the appearance of the world is not real in and of itself. However, it can be recognized as Brahman. In that, we recognize its true nature and reality.

In this book, Henry explores the many facets of Self realization and its progress into Nonduality. He emphasizes the so important point that Nonduality isn't about gathering concepts or beliefs or arguing who's right but is a direct recognition of our deeper nature.

Henry explores how we got caught in the content of experience and why that leads to suffering and karma, which are essentially unresolved experiences. He goes on to explore the way out and the rediscovery of our true, Nondual nature, behind the appearances of individuality and the world.

This is the difference between living in memory or living reality.
Davidya Buckland
Author, Our natural Potential
Courtney, BC January 2022

PREFACE

As a preface to this book, I would like to present the basic principles of Advaita/Nonduality teachings. The relative meaning of Nondual or Oneness may seem simple, but attempting to understand singularity as a quality or state from a spiritual context will only confuse the mind. The ordinary mind is habituated to experiencing the world as diverse. Even an encapsulating imagination of something abstract like the "human spirit" will eventually be lost in the apparent separateness of things. Therefore, a direct experience of the unifying value of Oneness that underlies and connects life is necessary to complement any understanding we may have.

Meditative practices that allow the mind to transcend thoughts and ideas bring us to a direct experience of Oneness, a state of emptiness free of thoughts, where even the body and sensations seem to disappear. The experience of Oneness during meditation and the mind's understanding of the experience brings about an initial awakening as to "Who am I." And the teachings of Nonduality play a vital role in helping us truly understand Oneness intellectually. The principles are easy to recognize and assimilate because they are how "nature" functions at the most intrinsic level. If one looks closely and investigates within, a recognition of the actual reality of self arises.

From the book:

Shankara's —*The Crest Jewel of Discrimination* by Swami Prabhavananda and Christopher Isherwood

The following are phrases I underlined some years ago and used as a guide to help recondition erroneous belief structures. As a spiritual seeker, I was inspired to read these passages whenever I could.

1. No object, no kind of knowledge, can be authentic if its existence is only temporary. Absolute reality implies permanent existence.

2. What then is Reality behind all our experiences? There is only one thing that never leaves us—deep consciousness. It alone is the constant feature of all backgrounds, and this consciousness is the authentic, absolute Self.

3. Shankara says that the world of thought and matter is not absolute; he does not mean it is non-existent. The world's appearance is and is not. It is a paradox going beyond the Mind's comprehension.

4. Maya's world appearance has its basis in Brahman, the eternal, infinite absolute. The concept of Maya applies only to the phenomenal world, which according to Shankara, consists of names and forms. It is non-existent, yet it differs from the Reality of Brahman upon which it depends for its existence.

5. The universe is a superimposition upon Brahman. Brahman remains eternally infinite and unchanged. It is not transformed into the universe. It simply appears as this universe to us in our ignorance. Superimposition is the apparent presentation to consciousness by the memory of something previously observed elsewhere.

6. Brahman is not an object of perception. Brahman is not non-objective in the absolute sense. For Brahman is the thing of the Ego-idea. We know it quite well by intuition that the

inner Self must exist since the Ego-idea is a presentation of the Self.

7. I am I, I am private, I am separate, I am an individual—we have set up a kind of chain reaction that makes further superimposition inevitable. The claim to individuality for ourselves implies uniqueness everywhere. It automatically superimposes multiple worlds of creatures and objects upon the one undivided reality, the Existence, Brahman. Ego-idea and world appearance depend on each other. Lose the Ego-idea in transcendental consciousness, and the world appearance must necessarily vanish.

8. Absolute freedom is not something to be attained, absolute knowledge is not something to be gained, Brahman is not something to be found. Only Maya is to be pierced, ignorance which has to be overcome. The process of discrimination is a process of negating, revealing the positive fact that our fundamental nature eternally exists. We are Brahman—and only that

From a contemporary perspective of Nonduality teachings:

1. Oneness as truth and unity is the underlying and permeating reality that connects life.

2. Oneness is veiled by the limitations of a mind/body organism living in ignorance of the true Self.

3. The veil is primarily the misidentification of the ego/mind projecting limitations of a separate self living in a separate reality. Known as Maya, or illusion from Indian texts, it is regarded as a concept to help understand that the relative and absolute is not a "thing."

4. The veil of ignorance is a long-standing behavioral reality set up by ancestral DNA and up-to-date conditioning passed down through generations and reinforced by current world views and circumstances.

5. The personal veil is composed of thoughts, ideas, and beliefs that your ego takes to be accurate and control your life under the constraint of limitations.

6. The personal veil of thoughts superimposes the notion that I am somebody, have a name and do things. While this is functional, it is not who you indeed are. You are the conscious awareness experiencing form and function. Your consciousness is free and unbounded, an observer of life unfolding.

7. Realization of the true Self is the first stage of spiritual Oneness—it is complete unto itself. It demands and requires nothing. It just is.

8. The entire Cosmos and beyond is Oneness, you are Oneness, and when the Self realizes the unity of all things, everything is none other than Self appearing as modulations of the Self.

It is said in spiritual circles that nothing changes in the relative field of life after Self-realization even though an appreciation of consciousness as the vast unbounded Self is revealed. It may be easy to dismiss the value of spiritual enlightenment, given that everything, the person you were and the things around you, remains the same. From a relative perspective, such a claim is valid. What significantly changes is that Self-realization brings about freedom and stability beyond words. A knowing that who you are is Eternal and Infinite. Life may go on relatively the same, and it is part of you, but you are not limited by it.

INTRODUCTION

The Oneness experience, conceptualized as an ultimate reality beyond any experience, has no origin. It is origin itself; it is absolute. It is not ascribed to any lineage, tradition, philosophy, or religion. It is an eternal truth, the unknown we all wish to know. Many throughout recorded history have come to realize Oneness from different journeys and relative points of view. "All roads lead to Rome" is a beautiful metaphor. However, choosing a smooth and rapid spiritual road may be challenging within today's complex and technological lifestyle and the subsequent prevalent quick fix societal attitudes.

The writing of this book represents my spiritual journey and how I have experienced Advaita or Oneness. I am a teacher of Transcendental Meditation and have practiced the technique along with the TM-Sidhi program for over 50 years. I'm currently involved with a small cohesive group of meditators, most of whom also began their spiritual journey in the practice of TM. We come together for online meditation daily and in scheduled retreat sessions. After our regular effortless meditation practice, we engage the meditative samadhi state with techniques to enliven the more profound, more refined fluctuations of consciousness. Samadhi is a gateway through consciousness where functioning from sublime and profound silence strengthens harmony and integration with nature at its origin.

Over the past 50 years, my spiritual path has integrated daily meditation with worldly endeavors. It has been liberating to realize consciousness on its primordial level and unfold everyday life. The spiritual journey arises in conversation, but self-realization is this very moment, and it is all we have. To truly recognize and experience the "present moment" is both unfathomable and yet so natural at the same time.

Questions about consciousness, one's state of awareness, and how it relates to personal reality rarely come to mind in the general population. Primarily, our daily experience is relatively routine. We wear it well. We embrace and take the worldly experience for granted; we call it life. A small percentage of people sense that there may be more to life and accept the challenge, and a need arises to deeply investigate questions close to our hearts.

I am just an ordinary guy who has also had extraordinary reality experiences for most of my life. When I was younger, I thought it was normal to be as big as the universe until my mother told me otherwise, and my brother laughed his head off. These experiences, which never diminished through the years, supported my spiritual endeavors when I became a spiritual seeker. They also sustained an evolutionary progression to validating an overall current reality of Self, untouched by conventional concepts of individuality, unaffected by anything but touches everything. As a result, I feel there is an appropriate natural pull to write about Advaita or Nonduality, the Oneness experience related to the ordinary human being's condition.

One common theme or principle in Advaita or Nondual teachings is that your conscious day-to-day experience of reality is what you make it. One's conscious awareness at any given timeline is an expressed personal reality filtered through your psychophysiological nervous system. Even though we share a consensus reality with billions of people on earth, your interpretation is unique. Truth is how we perceive it to be. Considering reality shifts moment to moment, albeit in a seemingly sequential continuity, every moment is on its own. What you see in front of you right now is your reality. No question. It does not matter about philosophical arguments about the nature of reality. What you are observing is your personal, intimate reality at any given moment.

I know it is common for spiritual teachers to say, and I say this myself, that an experience is an experience. They come and go. Pay little attention to experiences, do not hang on or get attached, and take them too seriously. It hinders progress is an accurate statement; we should see that any experience is an illusion. However, and as mentioned, when one understands reality at any moment, it is a reality to them; whether it is actual reality is up for discussion.

I have had many spiritual experiences, too many to relate, and they go back as early as infancy. I was an innocent, wide-eyed child where everyday out-of-body experiences and spacious awareness were the norms. There was a period during adolescence when I seemed to have lost the daily appreciation of the realm of consciousness. Still, I think it had more to do with growing up and trying to be the man society expected. It was not until my twentieth year that the clear experience of unbounded awareness returned. That was when I started Transcendental Meditation.

There was not a year or even months without incredible experiences of metaphysical or esoteric reality from that point forward. Under Maharishi Mahesh Yogi, the founder of the Transcendental Meditation Movement, I eventually gained a mature understanding of the spiritual experience. He always said these experiences belonged to the purification category, the release of stress in the psychophysiology appearing as perceptual experiences. He went on to say that some of these experiences can have a genuine value of the Divine, but until Unity Consciousness is realized, it is better to consider all these as "smoke." I still believe in this to a point, but somehow, I also know that in most of the experiences I had, there was always this openness and clarity of an unnameable presence. It wasn't so much a component of the experience but what held the experience. It is what I experience now as an abiding continuous perspective on reality. I also verified this from scripture, modern consciousness mapping, and more so these days by the many friends and associates on the spiritual journey. Having wow experiences, epiphanies, breakthroughs, and insights, whether it lasts a few minutes, hours, days, or weeks, are as valid as any temporal or sacred experience of life that one can have.

My last significant shift in consciousness occurred in the fall of 2019, and it showed up unexpectedly. The transition was instantaneous and gentle, a natural unfolding of a vast humbling reality dimension. One minute, my perspective was what it was. Then seamlessly, without fanfare, consciousness shifted into what I can only call a full love-bliss-realization of Unity or Oneness. Before this Unity shift, my consciousness experience was stand-alone as an absolute unbounded Self, a Oneness, but it seemed incomplete. I had attained this partial stage as a dominant reality only a few years earlier. The perspective was one of a partial fullness in appreciation of reality. Objective reality, the world around me, including my mind/body organism, was distinct and carried on as it always had. The infinite, unbounded Self was a witness or observer to all transpiring objectively. It was great that this unwavering stability in Self was untouched, but it was relatively dry. The liveliness and flow that spiritual adepts speak of were missing; therefore, it felt incomplete.

When Unity Consciousness, the wholeness of Oneness dawned, then the Self as consciousness was clearly seen and appreciated thoroughly within and as the other. Everything, I mean everything, was experienced as Self and was rolling in waves of love-bliss. Love was the connection between the Self and the other as one holistic consciousness, and the quality of love was beyond the human dimension. The Observer was the Observed, and the Observation process, this unifying quality of love was Self. It is difficult to describe the reality of wholeness where all the parts are seen as Oneness. It is virtually impossible. Language and concepts don't do this experience justice.

Over the weeks, the intensity of this shift in perspective integrated into a calmer reality, where the intense love-bliss subsided. However, there are still periods where intense bliss can arise, mostly in meditation. The love aspect is always there but more appreciated as attributes or qualities of love, such as feelings of friendliness, respect, gratitude, compassion, acceptance, happiness, and forgiveness. An actual and natural caring capacity arises when one sees everything as Self. Not that living in this stage of reality, Unity Consciousness, is one and done, not by a long shot. Unity consciousness is much more amiable and richer and untouched on one level by any ordinary circumstance. Everything is seen as Self, all are invited and welcome, but there is more to unfold along the spiritual journey.

Nevertheless, the individual living in the natural state of Unity is still closely tied with the collective conditioned existence. The interrelatedness—the intimacy among species or within nature goes far beyond any statement or words. Challenging and even adverse situations still arise because life's natural unfolding is closely tied to each other. And these challenges come unexpectedly; the variety of life is never-ending, especially in this period of global transition where a shift towards truth and spirituality is on the rise.

Introducing this book responds to the current global events shaping our planet. It is the summer of 2021 at the time of this writing, and I realize the energies apparent in the collective consciousness are polarizing more than ever before. I say this because I have been involved in the spiritual community since the flower power days of the sixties, where the concept of intimate feeling or sensing your way through life was introduced and promoted. And hooray for intuition; the more you focus on something, the more it becomes a part of you. I appreciate more the stirrings and movement of life energy individually and collectively as I have strengthened spiritually. Without exception, the energies swirling these days are of a magnitude that is waking up many people. And it does not have to be a full-blown self-realized spiritual awakening. Just noticing something is up, something is not quite resonating, or sitting well with life is an awakening. The sensing of self, relative to and placed in the context of a seen global arising of significant events, is the first sign to investigate further.

From this perspective, it is all the same universal flow of differentiated energy patterns. It is all inside one's larger Self, and the experience can be expressed on either the micro- or macro-level. It depends on the focus of attention in the unbounded field of awareness. I can feel great most days, content and apart from all the rumblings reported by the media. Often, I do not even get involved. Suddenly, unexpectedly, energy wells up inside. It calls out indecisiveness, division, uncomfortableness; some correction must occur. Where did that come from? It is unresolved energies, individual and collective crying out. It is accurate, it is now, and it is happening. From any specific uncomfortableness that may spontaneously occur, I find ease by normally processing this arising internally, using various techniques that allow expanding consciousness rather than its suppression and contraction. Then I will do a round of effortless meditation. After that, I may go for a bike ride and feel super energized, finding relative completion to distorted energies. I also find peace in that I have been contributing in some small part to balance the energies of global consciousness by going inwards, meditating, and promoting the rise in shared coherence for many years. Aside from individual meditation, I also involve myself in collective gatherings of group meditation techniques. These resonate powerfully with the wholeness and harmony of nature's actual reality of Oneness.

Life is doing what it does. Stay on track, stay out of the mud by looking after yourself; I have learned this through various teachings. I have followed the advice up to this point in my life. Do what you know to be right is the common theme. So far, I have directed a lot of that right doing to the Self in an individually oriented manner where the adage is; if you are a bright and beautiful green tree, you will contribute to the overall forest. Doing such personally and having faith helps, but it is not enough. There is a calling out there now like I experienced when I went on TM teacher training in the early 70s. It was more of a zealous goal to change the world through Yoga back then. It is different now; the cosmic energies feel heightened, not only from a personal perspective, but there is more at stake, judging by the world events over the past two decades.

What I have been experiencing lately in the past year has shifted my awareness to a greater understanding of what the personal events and circumstances in one's life come to signify on that energetic level. One must be ready and available to receive that which is apparent. It is not a matter of reading into anything or figuring out some scenario. It simply identifies signposts that carry, and they all do an energy signal. All events in one's life are there for a reason, and it is pretty easy to tap into; it is almost like following breadcrumbs that an invisible someone has left for you.

Interestingly enough, that invisible someone is yourself. It is your world, you make it what it is, and it always tells you something. It is not an indicator of good or bad; it is more an energy signal of either positively or negatively oriented polarity. When the feeling or intuition expands, a positive signpost shows that aligning with this thread will move towards wholeness. If it is a feeling or intuition of neutrality or contraction, and that does not mean it is wrong, it shows following this thread will end in a small self-oriented activity of limited value. It may also eventually become a good thing because nature will always move progressively forward again.

There were a few breadcrumbs, events that surfaced in my life starting about a year ago that got me to a place of authoring this book. It is one of the last things I thought would happen had someone asked me before a year ago. Not that writing is odd, or even the delivery of a book, it just seemed unlikely given the direction I was going at the time. It is key that life presents the opportunity, and clearly, choices are there to be made. What resonates the most is what is most relevant. Following this, I picked up on events that seemed to shine brighter for reasons unknown. It felt more like unconscious rather than conscious decisions were being made. To make a somewhat long story short, a string of synchronistic events guided me in feel-good energy that placed a choice in front of me to write or not write. A few months back, I began to journal my experience and motivation in that direction. And then, one day, a cascade of opportunity and clear seeing of aim emerged. Once I started, I initially shook my head, not because of lack of confidence, but not knowing what to expect as an outcome, and it became an outpouring. Writing was not like in high school or college; it seemed automatic, and it felt like I was reading my writing instead of planning thoughts and finding the keyboard.

It has been an extraordinary experience, and I owe the pointing in a positive direction, and the writing of this book, to one specific drop of a breadcrumb. That one typical wonderful human being is Kathy McClement. She inspired me and laid out reasoning with concrete steps forward to why this adventure would benefit us and the society we see caught up in a collective struggle these days. If you have ever met a pure soul and a self-assured woman all in one, well, it is such a pleasure and joy.

I am writing this book to bring awareness and the knowledge of Unity to those who will read this book. I am also launching a website, advaitaspeaks.com. I intend this portal to offer a practical application of Nondual spiritual teachings and healing modalities. Primarily a Blogspot, there are formulae available for encouraging the growth and development of the spiritual soul in all of us. The instructions are centuries old, if not more, as are the healing techniques, but the commitment is to place a fresh modern spin and provide positive enhancement in the unfoldment of conscious awareness. It is there to realize the full potential inherent in the human being. It may have seemed difficult in the past, but the cosmic energies surrounding our planet currently make it more conducive to achieving self-actualization.

With this book and the website, I am putting together what I feel is an easily understood expression of the simple Advaita principles of Self as an ongoing process. As mentioned, this is not new. However, it is a compilation of teachings gained through my 50+ years of being devoted to reaching Moksha, liberation, the state of enlightenment, and recognizing that more is continually unfolding. A recognition the journey never ends.

In the last sections of this book, I will foray into Brahmanand Divinity. The supreme unnameable grace and joy of Divine Mother, the feminine aspect of existence that has been at the forefront and occupying human consciousness more so this century. All the stages of consciousness reality are potentially available to any human being. We could consider these higher stages the pinnacle of consciousness expansion relative to the time/space continuum we inhabit on earth at present. They go beyond my Unity Consciousness reality and the full appreciation of a greater lived reality. I have had glimpses, brushes of something I can only describe as Truth. My existential reality of Unity is beckoning from my current stage, calling me to investigate further into what lies deep within the unbounded ocean of consciousness; it feels natural and automatic, call it an evolutionary force of nature. To discuss and elucidate these higher stages of consciousness, I will rely on two long-standing and reliable sources who started their spiritual journey in earnest during the early 70s. They have embodied higher stages of consciousness and developed international exposure through lecturing and writing on the themes of consciousness and spirituality as the primary reality. It is pretty exciting what awaits the human experience if we can, as a collective, or better yet the governing bodies, find the will to transition into something available, natural, and effective for the betterment of humanity. Shivada Amrita, Aug. 27, 2021

I. PRECEPTS AND TENETS OF NONDUALITY

Nondual philosophy teachings from Advaita Vedanta have a long-known history dating back to the holy Master Adi Shankara (509-497 BCE). These teachings are part of the Vedic Period of India, which has written records and a lineage of spiritual teachers dating back to (1300- 900 BCE). It is an excellent storyline in time. Adi Shankara, a simple boy, leaves home at an early age and goes on to realize Self, the ultimate truth of reality, the Oneness that underlies and permeates all things. Self-realization back then was a lived reality, well known, and embedded in the culture of that time.

Later in his life, Adi Shankara established the four seats of knowledge in India, one in each cardinal direction. It was during a period in history when the land required revival of the Vedic heritage and accompanying systems of gaining knowledge. It still stands today as a testament to the depth and endurance of his teaching. His consummate writing, *The Crest Jewel of Discrimination,* is a gem of spiritual knowledge expressing and holding the truth of Advaita/ Vedanta or Nonduality to this day.

We were introduced to this book back in the late 60s when another revival of spiritual knowledge was unfolding, the adoption of Yoga as a mainstream meditation practice in the West. The book provided knowledge about the concepts of Nonduality and how it relates to spiritual progress in light of the Vedic literature expressing the Oneness of Reality.

We were all on a course with Maharishi Mahesh Yogi, the founder of Transcendental Meditation. Mostly, we were very one-pointed on his teachings of the Science of Creative Intelligence. The Science of Creative Intelligence was a course Maharishi had structured to introduce westerners to some of the underlying principles of life and spiritual evolution. Maharishi drew these principles from the ancient Vedic Texts. Adi Shankara and his writings on Advaita were from that lineage of Vedic seers and scholars, as was the Maharishi, so we read as many related Indian philosophy texts as possible that echoed Maharishi's teachings.

Of course, many have followed in Adi Shankara's footsteps outside the lineage of Holy Vedic Masters, including the venerable and well-known sages, such as Ramakrishna, Vivekananda, Sri Aurobindo, Ramana Maharshi, Sri Nisargadatta Maharaj, Krishnamurti, and other enlightened seers up to this present day. Some contemporary teachers who have investigated and brought awareness to Nondual teachings are Ramesh Balsekar, Ram Dass, Alan Watts, Adyashanti, Rupert Spira, Jean Klein, Joseph Campbell, Fred Davis, and the list goes on. These are just a few who have impacted the spiritual community with their teaching style.

It is so curious to see that the teachings of Nonduality are essentially the same Truth, but the individuals who teach possess and impart varied styles and personalities. I am not here to give an in-depth historical account of their lives and teachings. The many Nondual teachers today spreading the truth of Advaita from their perspective are all well documented. I will refer to them occasionally, but I believe my approach, which may appear similar, has some new views when combined with the ageless knowledge of Vedic literature. This book offers a combination of Nonduality recognition, the Oneness experience, and a taste of Indian philosophy. In addition, I include some modern insights and techniques which apply to consciousness-raising.

From the translation of the original texts to the modern interpretation of nonduality handed down over the centuries, the message is simple, straightforward, and easily misunderstood. There is Oneness—and only Oneness. The mind has difficulty because it is so simple and close that the limited ego can only see Oneness as something. Our mind and intellect are accustomed to objectifying, distinguishing, and thus separating. It considers the entirety of creation as isolated, solid things. We perceive from the viewpoint of separation. Perceiver, and the perceived. Subject and Object: Duality/Two-ness.

> From the identified ego, the view is diversity, and then awakening creates the simplest duality: consciousness and the world that emerges in Unity. However, subtle dualities remain that become resolved in Brahman.　　　—David Buckland

The Oneness of this entire creation—beholds—as if it were something apart from the seeing. This appearance of "apart" is the seeing from separation, from a dualistic perspective of **I am,** and I see Oneness based on my perception of conceptual reality. The fact of what my experience presents to me as a separate entity. Whereas, Oneness, seen through the lens of Oneness, means that the individual perceiver and the perception are Oneness since the act of perceiving is all that there is. There is clear recognition from simply perceiving that there is only one thing going on here: who you most deeply are—consciousness, the all-ness. It is a genuine paradox because all these parts imply many and seem separate, but Oneness only appears differentiated. It's hard for the mind to grasp fully, if at all.

Suppose one steps beyond the mind's conceptual protocol and simply appreciates Oneness on an intuitive feeling level. Then this "One" magnificent, altogether movement of living wholeness in constant motion is "you" and "you are it." When seen from this pure state of being, the being of existence, that feeling we all carried from birth, it is the pure act of constant unbroken perceiving of the arising of the ever-unfolding present moment. These are words that may come close to doing justice to the description of Oneness, Advaita.

> Oneness is always your experience, and if you think that you do not have the Oneness experience, it is because you feel that you are something other than Oneness. Is that even possible?　　—Fred Davis

Oneness—what does that mean practically? Oneness, as a singularity? Objects of singularity carry an essence of oneness from a scientific perspective, and so far, only theorized in the applied Quantum Field Theory of Physics. It is known as the "field effect" of various dimensionalities of increasing subtle subatomic particles, all finding expression from a single unified field application. And it all comes down to the idea of Source, source of creation, the inherent Big Bang.

Wholeness is another interpretation of Oneness. From a metaphysical perspective, wholeness is greater than the sum of the parts. What is that more significant aspect or value given to the meaning of wholeness? How can one even appreciate it experientially? Even on an intellectual level? And what might it truly mean for us in the larger picture of humanity going forward? And how does that ephemeral idea of wholeness relate to the singularity of Source?

The limited mind cannot know the essence of Oneness from a worldly perspective, metaphysical, or even a spiritual one. Reason cannot pierce to the core of the underlying singularity within the objective world. It is just a form and phenomenon for the ego, with an attached label or arbitrary consensus of meaning. The nature of Oneness is postulated as pure consciousness in spiritual terms from ancient texts. It is experiential reality passed down through the ages to anyone ready to see the truth. The limited mind does not know pure consciousness directly. The closest the ego/mind gets is a sense of it—I am aware, conscious—a sense of being. It is a conceptual interpretation of an Absolute State of Knowing for the mind. I know consciousness exists because I am self-aware.

It is somewhat convincing with wholeness on a conceptual level; the totality of the sum of the parts is simply Source expressing itself as the many. Source as Oneness, and Oneness as many. Ultimately it transcends all meaning because the conceptual mind cannot go beyond the concept. It cannot know the abstract value of wholeness. It can just be **It** as an expression of integrated self-awareness— consciousness becoming or shining as that value of Wholeness/ Source. It's a paradox for sure, the material realm as it is known and the absolute field of pure potentiality that the mind cannot understand. How do they connect at Source, and what would that knowledge be like in practical terms for humans occupying planet Earth and the Cosmos at large?

> Nonduality is quite simple and can be described in a few sentences: Picture a coin spinning on its edge on a table. The coin represents source energy. One side of the coin is blank, indicating the potentiality inherent in Source. On the other side of the coin is the face of God, manifested reality. The coin is spinning at an incredibly high rate. All you see are blurred lines melding into a holographic sphere. What do you see in that vision? Oneness, both sides of the coin, are expressions of reality. Absolute and relative in Unity, Non-Duality. —Cornelius Christopher

Dawning and Development of Dualism

Most people on this planet live their lives in a supposedly "normal" waking state. It is a life of being a subject moving about in a world of objects. It is a world full of forms as far as one can see or even imagine. It exists based on a particular level of conditioned information. We move through life, referring to ourselves as **I am. I am here, I am sentient,** and **I am this body.** This **I am** is referenced to doing, seeing, and interacting with objects outside of that sense or sphere of the pure **I** as a distinct subject. This is where the problem of genuinely recognizing the actual reality of all things begins.

> When the notion of "I am" is gone, the complete withdrawal into "oneself" is what remains. "I am" is a conceptual state; when it is dropped, only Brahman, true "Absolute I," remains.
>
> —Siddharameshwar

It is not how we perceived the world when we were born. The moment of sentience occurred sometime in the developmental stages in the womb. Some metaphysical arguments report that the owner has occupied when the house is fully built. When the fetus has fully developed somewhere in the third trimester, the soul, the Jiva, individuated personal Atman, hosts the body.

There is an emotional awareness in the interplay within itself in this sentience, not knowing that it is subject itself, outside of the simple awareness of being, pure awareness of being. Sensations are somewhat muted, as are the other faculties of mind during this crucial period of the nervous system coming online: neuron circuitry and further organ development. The communication integration systems must process and deliver mind/body information. You could say it is the pure arising of consciousness aware of stimuli without recognizing what that stimulus is. It's all just happening within this space of a fetus or baby's awareness. You could rightly say this is an early state of Nondual Reality—the emergence of consciousness alone through an individual mind/body organism.

Gradually through repeated stimuli that are happening 24/7 and the development of the nervous system apparatus to an optimal level, the information conditioning absorbed by the baby is being imprinted and saved in consciousness and the other corresponding frequency vibrations of the nervous system and energy centers. Form and phenomena become realized as distinct reoccurring events within the awareness of the baby. Through time and further development of the infant into childhood, a real sense of the reality of the perceptions takes hold.

It is still occurring without a sense of separation. It is just one homogeneous movement of activity in motion. Of course, the infant recognizes its body and parts, but not in the identified sense that this is my body. All of this changes as the infant develops into the child and to different stages of development. The deep imprinting starts soon enough through repeated conditioning, primarily done by the parents and near family, expressing their reality to the infant. It all begins here; a closeness or immediate self-awareness of the environment, primarily the body, comes online. The reference point of that conscious awareness begins to be imprinted with **I am the body**. It's all fine and well at this stage, and for some time, as everything, all the baby's needs are taken care of; this is not to say that all babies, infants, and children share a safe and secure environment.

> Once you free yourself of the idea, **I am the body,**
> and the consequences of this idea, you will awaken
> to your natural state of being.   —Jean Klein

With **I am the body,** the **I am** is the foremost individuated conditioning, where conscious awareness is perceiving through boundaries or limitations imposed by the mind. A human mind is an incredible tool that navigates this material world and holds all the faculties necessary to live life as an expression of the fullness of life through creative, intelligent design. The problem arises during periods of linear time/space continuum when the energies required for the whole dynamic representation of these faculties are dampened. We are through natural cyclical forces living in a period of lowered vibration. It is like the cycles of the weather. The Sun is always there, but clouds and storms get in the way.

> Become conscious of becoming conscious, say or think I am, and add nothing to it! Be aware of the stillness that follows the I am. Sense your presence and the naked, unveiled unclothed beingness. It is untouched by young or old, rich or poor, good or bad, or any other attributes.
>
> —Ramana Maharishi

The faculties inherent in the mind are the five senses, feelings and emotional response, the intellect in its discriminating value, and the development of the ego—the individuated sense of self. Small innocent children formulate the world around them through their life experiences and the ongoing conditioning constantly coming their way. As mentioned, this depends on the time/space location of the dominant universal energies of creation, maintenance, and dissolution. Are these forces present in synergy and balance or distorted by the natural cosmic flow of changing cycles within a cycle dictating time? These resulting universal energies in a seemingly random but specifically oriented space/time continuum collection are expressed materially as our mind/body organism.

More precisely, from a limited ego perspective, in Sanskrit called Pragyapradh, the **I am, I am my thoughts, and I am the body** arises because of what is called in Vedic Knowledge the "mistake of the intellect." Maharishi Mahesh Yogi lectured extensively on this topic of Pragyapradh when dealing with consciousness becoming conscious. The "mistake of the intellect" is also discussed in *The Crest Jewel of Discrimination,* an apt title for Adi Shankara's book. The most illustrious self-effulgent knowing by the intellect can within that knowledge, be that knowing through discernment, and realize the ultimate truth of Advaita/Vedanta, Nonduality.

A resolute intellect eventually approaches this Oneness. However, within the time/space continuum cycles, human intelligence exhibits variations of energy frequencies. And Pargyapradh, "the mistake of the intellect," is due to a shallow energy vibration cycle where the point value of mind/body expressed radiates imbalance and distortions. These are mirrored in the dynamics of the mechanics of nature—evolutionary forces in tilt. The translation of Pragyapradha means Pragnya/intellect and apradh/ crime. The culprit is when the intellect mistakes or becomes overshadowed by material consciousness and loses connection with the wholeness of consciousness. It is the dawning and development of dualism in one's life.

> A personal me attempting to think about what I am
> is a fatally flawed activity from the outset. There is
> no real personal me here that could either think or
> fail to think. The entire story of a personal me is
> just an unowned, conditioned thought stream. That
> thought stream is itself conditioning. —Fred Davis

What is being absorbed by the mind in a time/space continuum of low and distorted energies is mostly non-truth. Coupled with material influences through the constant conditioning of the mind, which is not necessarily of a wholistic spiritual and loving nature, the distortion is complete. The ego becomes identified with this material world, and the first impact is the emergence of **I am the body,** and there is an environment apart from me. The arrival of a world that abounds with polarity. A spectrum of events and circumstances bombards the ego and is embedded in the subconscious mind's storehouse of impressions. These impressions or conditioning are re-visited as programs in the conscious mind of individual awareness. Relative to the activity we undertake or the path traveled by the individual, the stored conditioned response will vary in scope and intensity.

> The primary problem is with the misidentification of the actual source of subjectivity and the presumption that it is local rather than nonlocal. In the process of spiritual discovery, one looks to discover what it is aware of and has the authority to sense the existence of I-ness, rather than a specific or circumscribed me, as the I.   —David Hawkins

Unfortunately, the other part that plays a massive role in the corruption of a person's pure awareness or consciousness is passed down DNA/Genetic material from parents and ancestors. The passed down information genome may come with flaws or coding that are subnormal or distorted in sequence. It may add to the malaise of the up-to-date conditioning that the ego/mind/intellect misinterprets by simply identifying or attaching invalid meaning to **I am**. Hereditary and current life experiences inevitably lead to a base perception and perspective of reality that do not hold the highest truth. The instilled base perspective is of separateness, a subject/object relationship distinct from one another: duality, two-ness. Nonduality is simple: dualism is complex.

> Your mind will use any material from your life to drain your attention from the present moment. The mind does not exercise quality control; it will throw up stories and feelings from your past or imagined future to prevent you from directing your attention elsewhere. Mind constantly presents the past or the future as the present.   —Jac O'Keefe

This description of nonduality and the brilliant wording of Jac O'Keefe is still all conceptual. It is unfortunate, but it is the mind. Even from a cosmic sense of self-realization, the best and most accurate descriptive language only defines Oneness. On the other hand, reading these passages from a relatively cosmic mind perspective, the energy imprinted in the writing of the words can be intuited in resonance and allow for a clearer intellectual understanding of the writer's intention.

Let's say that someone understands Nondual reality from reading these passages to whatever degree and has some appreciation or awakening to the vast glory of Oneness. What does that mean to that person? Suppose this reality of Oneness is lived consciously, and consciousness knows itself as the unity of all things. In that case, life expression is perfect within this ease and natural comfort of living. We may experience that nothing matters; life is unfolding as it should, in the majesty of Oneness. What a relief, nothing matters, nothing to change, but even so, everything does impeccably count. Everything is precious, so Nonduality is not a negating of life—it is that which brings more Divine qualities forward.

Adi Shankara and all the Advaita teachers point to the holiness of life. That inexplainable power behind this 3-D world we live and inhabit. We feel it when the attention is being directed towards the spiritual realm. Sometimes we know it through direct experience and epiphanies. However, we often ignore it out of practical rationalization to maintain a consensus reality, which we call sanity, but this is nothing other than ignorance.

> Questions arise about the source of the capacity to realize existence or beingness and whether such qualities are innate or superimposed by silent paradigm presumptions. One may ask, "By what quality does the abstract even become discernable? And is not that knowingness itself merely a higher level of abstraction?" Again, although these queries may seem academic to the intellect, experientially, they are a priority and profoundly transformative as the light of the levels of consciousness. At the

highest levels, they represent the last clouds that
hide the radiance of the sun of Divinity.
—David Hawkins

Nonduality. There is only Oneness. In the beginning, there is
pure potentiality resting as a Source. From a metaphysical perspective,
the Source describes the field of all possibilities in potential, a state
of Oneness. Current scientific thinking agrees on a unifying field
at the Planck scale, but the inherent qualities of the field in relation
to manifest creation are yet under investigation. Source energy is
motivated by Universal Will, or scientifically by the field dynamics
of bosons and fermions interacting and materializing into the
many as **what is,** refers to creation. **What is,** arises as just that, the
experience or occurrence present at any given moment, from any
given perspective. Changing this understanding intellectually in
search of miracle answers in the material world or modifying them
through research may have some temporary effect; finding solutions
to benefit humanity is a good thing, as we have seen through history.
However, the futility and vanity of ego's attempts to rationalize
existence at its core materially is like rearranging the furniture on
the Titanic or trying to Feng-shui the universe.

As an individual or collective, we can self-improve to a point and
feel good about it, but in the larger picture and scheme of things
in life, **what is,** continues to roll out in an eternal outpouring of
changing realities. One should not strive to find ultimate answers
to understand the individual and their role in creation from the
material perspective. The relative complexity of action and causality
is unfathomable; the primary perspective looks towards a higher
truth in reality from consciousness.

If you want to understand something from the human domain,
then try to understand the actual reality of a limited mind/ego
complex, the base cause of a distorted reality. Thanks in large
part to an ego-centric mind, your subconscious, that vast field
of unknown reality hidden to your person and the world around

you, is covered over by the notion or illusion of a fragmented individuality. For hundreds of years, it has been taken for granted that modern society believes the value of the subconscious mind is insignificant and thereby non-functional to relative existence. This unconscious awareness is an ever-present reality hidden temporarily and unknowingly and is always projected as an autonomic function within who you are. Through Nonduality teachings and meditative practice, your unconscious awareness will awaken and come online. To whatever degree, a new perspective will dawn, and even a glimpse can be life-altering. Therein lies the beginning realization of Self.

The automatic gathering and dispersal of information by the ego/mind complex from birth to the present heralds an acquired perceptive reality based on limitations. Ancestral genetic and natal DNA/genome expression and the subsequent up-to-date conditioning that follows are all stored as memory in the vast subconscious, which limited ego/mind misidentifies as reality.

Suppose one can genuinely understand Consciousness as Self and all-pervading, a lived experience. In that case, it can be seen the material reality we all experience is just an expression of Consciousness or Source energy. If one has a feel for that source, the awareness of living as the essence of existence, then one can have a real sense of the **Is-ness** of Consciousness as primary. If you quiet the mind a little, you will touch that sense of being. This touch reveals a calm stillness, a deep awareness that is most often generated by the heart. It leads to recognizing that your world is Oneness; the Self is all around you. Moreover, this recognition may result in seeing **what is** appearing as none other than a projection of your mind/ego complex. This is an opening to experience reality as a progression into an unknown mystery of life unfolding—the Oneness of you.

Through the whole trajectory from birth to childhood to adolescence and then into adulthood, we change so much, not only physically but also emotionally and intellectually. Yet something remains unchanged. That sense of something untouched is the eternal spark of life within. In the beginning, it may be felt like a very subtle, almost incomprehensible intuition. Still, when we bring our full attention to that felt intuition of what has been the same, there all along throughout our whole life, then that tiny seed of divine radiance can begin to reveal itself, can start to shine brighter and brighter in our lives. —Adyashanti

Oneness includes everything. I mean everything – subject/object, time/space continuum. There is no separation: someone over here seeking something over there does not exist, it is just a dream. For oneness, there is no possibility for something else, and there is nothing over there. THIS IS IT.

—Fred Davis

II. THE DISGUISE, THE PITFALLS AND BLESSINGS OF IGNORANCE: MIND AND EGO STRUCTURE

The ego is not an entity. Full stop. It is not a being with a personality and choices to be made. It's a collection of thoughts and ideas of who you are, and they are jostling for position, for supremacy among themselves. Am I the best I can be? Indeed, I'm better. Or I'm the victim and seek solace in comforting attention. These are just two ends of mind energy polarity that the ego can internalize. And wait until it goes on display with other social egos. We've all seen these behaviors but hardly recognize them clearly within ourselves. The ego is nobody. It is a competing set of programming. There is never rest from the ego because it knows no rest. Its main inherent program is to be active. It is the dynamism opposed to the stillness, the resting side of Being.

The ego/mind is the faculty of labeling and taking a standing position; it constantly gives meaning and categorizes the distinctions in the world of activity. The ego is a well-known phenomenon and can be studied and known by its inherent dynamics. The ego is that part of the mind that is claiming and identifying. I am doing this. I am doing that. Right now, I am presenting myself in this situation and circumstance. The ego identifies with stories from the past, carries them forward to the present, projects them into an expected future, and thereby feels in control.

In reality, it is like a lucid dream. The dream is the activity playing itself out, and the characters are just part of the script. There is no individual doer, and it is just happening. Believing in the reality of our imagination or dream is the only limitation. It is a set of entrenched habits of thought. These habits of thought are then re-enforced by up-to-date conditioning stored in the subconscious, along with the ancestral propensities that arise in symbiotic resonance with any triggered activity.

Limited ego is the product of the mind's conflict with reality. Ego/mind with a limited capacity to give true meaning to life justifies its superficial control built on a false reality. Confronting reality is the complex question of consciousness, the present state of individual awareness. Is it the product of materialism? Or is it primary and gives rise to manifest creation? The materialists believe that nothing exists except the phenomenal world as we perceive it and that all matter can explain existence through science. Over the centuries, scientific research and investigation have focused on measuring the surface values of importance and their inner realities. Materialists postulate that self-awareness or consciousness is a product of the modifications of matter, primarily the brain and nervous system interacting.

The importance of consciousness as a philosophical idea has been around longer than the emergence of scientific methodology to explain reality. Cases in point are the Vedic heritage and literature, Greek philosophy, and several other early eastern and western religions. The philosophical belief established was validated through experiential reality, and the conclusion is that consciousness is all there is. Everything is consciousness and nothing else. Modern science attempted to put that theory to rest by asserting that factual truth can only be verified through objective, repeatable verification—materialism. Slowly but surely, when scientific exploration turned the page from Newtonian physics to Quantum Field Theory, a shift in thought arose sometime around the early 1900s. The discovery of quantum electrodynamics has led to the present-day Unified Field Theories, which include the study of consciousness as a reputable scientific endeavor explored by some of the top scientists in the world.

Somewhere deep inside, there lies a sense, a whisper, of an actual reality that underlies and hums in every sentient being. The limited ego/mind is afraid of this recognition because it would be the death of its integrity and control. The paradox of this conflict is that the ego/mind, in its origin and function, can never know the unbounded reality of consciousness and will never know it but marches on as if one day it will. Therefore, the ego/mind born of this limited view of not fully understanding or knowing actual reality begins to label and identify with life, expressing as it does. It takes control or ownership as the doer to make sense and give meaning to the hard questions of Who? What? Where? When? Why? and How? For the most part, it does a miserable job because of its limited vision. This identification functionality does not reflect the infinite, unbounded reality. The final analysis projects a self that is nothing more than an illusion, a dream mind in a dream world. Whether the dream exhibits success or misery, it doesn't matter. It is an illusion covering a deeper, more fundamental reality. Even though one may call it an illusion, progress is being made individually in the evolutionary direction from some relative perspective. The ever-positive impulse of creative intelligence inherent in that fundamental reality guides the self towards fulfillment in whatever expression.

The limited ego/mind cannot capture the true reality of life, the natural flow of consciousness. It makes a mistake after mistake in its perception of truth, leading to a perspective that can only appreciate a small percentage on average of what the wholeness of life offers. Capturing actual reality is highly ironic because the ego/mind is all about grasping, identifying, and finding meaning. Still, its limits are in and of the material world. If only the status of the mind would become cosmic, then consciousness could shine forth within and without limitations in all its unbounded glory. Then this ego/mind would be released from the seeming attachment and control it portrays.

This vision of possibilities awaits the limited unaware individual ego/mind. Then all actions are the actions of the Universe. All desires are God's desires moving through us. God's will moves every atom in the universe and all that exists, and nothing can act without that power. There is nowhere you can stand outside the causal structure of life and not be part of it. **You are it.** Divinity will always be acting through the apparent you.

The mind labels every objective expression of reality to know it. From a survivalist standpoint, this was very useful and necessary to remember, label, categorize, give meaning, and act from that remembrance in the event of life-threatening circumstances during days of the hunter/gatherer period. Survival instincts served us well in those times, and this survival energy is directly related to human's lower chakra energy centers. Ancient metaphysical science describes seven energy centers in the body known as chakras. At times regarded as a myth, the function of the chakras is to draw upon universal energy to sustain spiritual, mental, emotional, and physical health. These chakra centers located from the base of the spine to the top of the brain have unique energy qualities. They provide a system of energy points within a conscious reality that affects our well-being when active to whatever degree.

The Root chakra, the first energy center, is located at the perineum. It is related generally to physical survival, stability, and health. The second, the Sacral chakra, is located near the navel area and represents emotions, sexuality, and vitality. The third energy center, the Solar Plexus chakra, indicates personal power, action, and manifesting. As evolution in the human species progressed, the second chakra energy center became more dominant. It resulted in the ego perceiving the world around oneself not so much threatened by unexpected danger, but now with a growing sense of the personal self and its relation to tribe or community. The first and second energy centers were online together in their varying dominance since relatedness to others was still based upon survival.

> The ego is not the real you; it was inherited as part of being born a human. It basically originates from the animal world. The evolution of consciousness happened through the primitive stages of mankind's evolution, so it could be said that seeking enlightenment is to recapitulate the history of human development.
>
> —David Hawkins

Most egos currently express and live from the dominant third chakra energy, the one of personal expression, how to fit into society, and how to appear to people around me. How can I gain superiority and position higher in the social structural hierarchy? Interestingly, this chakra, the Solar Plexus, is in tune with the energies of the Sun, the dominant life force in this solar system. As humans, we are from the Solar Dynasty.

This current third chakra energy dominance is where today's world's problems started centuries ago when evolutionary forces tapped their activation energies. Look at the overall situation on this planet and place it squarely on the selfish behavior of a limited ego looking for superiority and trying to climb to the highest reaches of material value in an attempt to satisfy the search for Self. The ego/mind seeks the true meaning of an endeavor to find fulfillment, which unfortunately will never occur when the search is only in the realm of material gain. It is an imaginary path because of its instability and changeability. What is constantly changing and temporary can never be defined as the truth or provide lasting fulfillment.

The Heart chakra energy center is the fourth in line up the scale in consciousness-altering energies that can be fully activated or awakened in the human psychophysiology. It represents the qualities of love for self and others, the epitome of compassion. This absolute unifying quality of heart is next to energize dominantly in the collective and presumably bring about significant changes on the planet. The fifth is the Throat Chakra, which deals with the recognition of truth brought about by the opening of the heart and communication of that truth—speech, from the level of knowledge of the integrated Self. The sixth chakra center, sometimes called the Third Eye, has to do with the blossoming of intuition and universal guidance. The seventh, or Crown Chakra, is the opening of the lotus petals of highest realization, starting with inspiration and the spiritual connection of realized Self—the Atman and its universal liberation in Brahman. Brahman, all that is, source and causation, absolute ultimate reality, totality. As stated, and as a collective, we are currently ruled by the dominant third chakra, the ego/mind, and the identification with the material world is profound in the current reality. But eternally hidden behind and within every surface, every atom is the infinite Brahman, Oneness.

The natural movement of the mind is towards fulfillment. Still, by receiving false suggestive data due to the ego's misidentification with reality, the individual produces actions that are very familiar in the scheme of the limitations of the manifested universe, namely separation, and constraint. This movement, however, is parallel to the fundamental dynamics of pure consciousness or Source, expressing its potentiality as apparent separation to know itself. The initial stirring of consciousness to become conscious and Being becoming manifest. It is the underlying dynamics of creation, hidden in every expression of the progression of evolution.

The function of the mind is no different. The same inherent laws of creation have governed it since time immemorial. The only difference between the mind/ego in control, rather than the spontaneity of Source Eternal, is the mind/ego cannot reach a final and satisfactory conclusion to life because it is only an activation principle. It only sees the world from its viewpoint of limitations and identification. It is a function or tool for awareness to experience relativity, not the unbounded power and glory within, guiding every moment and movement.

Modern scientific investigation, especially physics, has deeply delved into ever subtler layers of physical nature to understand the functioning of the laws of nature. A unified field has been theorized, pointing to an emergent interactive process. Constituents of physical matter are seen repeatedly as potential in the superposition of photons simultaneously acting like waves and particles. Here, there, everywhere arising and disappearing paired or singular instantaneously. Amazingly, research has also shown that the dynamics of observation influence the nature of the observed. Namely, any investigation affects the outcome. It extended further to offer the same paradoxical characteristic behavior with electrons, atoms, and molecules.

The fundamental emergence of Source Energy as postulated by science has convinced many in this field of work that consciousness is primary and the material world, even though solid in appearance, is illusory due to its ever-changing nature based on the observer. Carl Jung, a foremost and eminent psychologist, described this dynamic of emergence when he talked about the heart of the expressed human ego concerning the subconscious. The defined value of limited ego-self is but a small portion of the total potential of Self-consciousness that the human possesses and can express—a vast unified field of possibilities, emergent qualities, and properties within the subconscious or Soul expression.

From a spiritual standpoint, the limited ego/self conceptualizes and labels its view and becomes that reality. Truth, hidden in plain sight by physical identification, lies beneath this phenomenal objectivity derived by the mind. However, this is often too sublime to be appreciated. Experience of the surface level of solid objects is limited to acquiring the actual value or nature inherent in the objective world we see around us. Creative Intelligence lies within the objective realm, and the mechanics of nature are revealed to an expanded consciousness. Today, one dreams of categorized labels and prescribed meanings produced by ego/mind. Release yourself from this identification and attachment, live a Nondual reality of

Self, in and as freedom. This eternal reality abides in the pure awareness or consciousness of Oneness, or Source-energy.

> Once you realize that all comes from within, that the world in which you live has not been projected on to you, but by you, your fear comes to an end. It's only when you fully accept responsibility for the little world in which you live and observe the process of its creation, preservation, and dissolution that you may be free from your imaginary bondage.
> —Nisargadatta Maharaj

This actual Nondual reality is beyond the ego/mind structure. It is always present, eternal, and unchanging. It is the seat of awareness within and around you; it is your authentic Self and does not care about relative ideas or beliefs. You are this unchanging, non-doing reality that is so near to you, and you miss it altogether. It is the eyes you see with, and simply the inherent awareness that you exist. It is that mystery of aliveness that you possess and express continually. All things everywhere are a part of this mystery of existence, consciously or not.

Seen through a self of intimate introspection, subtlest feelings, arises a sense of being, stillness, presence, the aliveness of awareness. This awareness, this consciousness, is the container of all physical objects, concepts, ideas, beliefs, labels, memory, and any meaning arising as identification and attachments. The ego/mind requires this identification to sustain itself when trying to understand life. And it's an ever-turning hamster wheel going nowhere fast.

Within spiritual progress, the unfoldment of actual reality is one of "forgetting is the remembering" and is the paradox of enlightenment. One must go beyond the apparent reality of the world of objectivity, which is illusory, but appearing as ever so solid that who would deny its existence? To find the essence, which underlies and permeates all things, is a matter of completely forgetting the

I am principle. One starts with relinquishing **I am someone; I am this** with scores of identities, and the **other,** people, places, and things that seemingly stand separate. This separation is but an illusion within the **totality** of the universal environment. You, your true Self, are the environment, all of it.

There is a natural progression to a higher energy frequency beyond the limited ego/mind; it has been slowly evolving through linear time and was initially formulated out of the survival energy chakra. A higher energy field is established when the Heart chakra begins to dominate with the cessation of control by the finite ego. However, not much has changed over thousands and thousands of years to date. There have been bright lights shining wisdom and truth over the centuries, and of course, material and technological comforts in life have flourished for some and at the dire expense of others. The overall appreciation of spiritual reality has often been dismal, only appreciated on the surface levels without a notion of what rests within as a more profound reality when the heart chakra fully opens.

> When you see that the mind invents everything,
> all will vanish. The good will vanish, the bad will
> vanish, and you will remain as you are.
> —Ramana Maharishi

The limited ego/mind will change its form or costume to meet different circumstances and situations. Indeed, the ego/mind is a tool to reference tangible manifest reality and place it into content and meaning. What has been conditioned from birth, the structural DNA expression, and the up-to-date conditioning of oneself, will reveal how the ego categorizes and responds to events and activities. The ego looks for evidence to prove its belief in the conditioned impressions held by the subconscious mind to exist in an imaginary world it believes is nearly complete and only requires an ego-self projected manipulation to guide the personal me forwards.

Because the ego is constructed of positionalities, it has no option to be anything else except what it is. It, therefore, becomes an inescapable source of endless suffering and loss. Above all else, it fears the future and the specter of death itself, which is intrinsic to the ego's structure.

—David Hawkins

Pure awareness exists out of time, with no boundaries or limitations. It is your Nature. It is always present and available now to have insight into the true nature of Reality. The environment around you, including the body/mind organism, is part and parcel of immediate consciousness. It is the relative expression of the creative process of pure consciousness from an internalized program that the individual and collective mind present.

The little **I am** seeking to enhance itself by external means of approval, external possessions, and external "love." The self that God created is whole, and it needs nothing. It is forever complete, safe, loved, and loving. It seeks to shape rather than get, extend rather than project. It has no needs and wants. It moves to join with others out of mutual awareness of abundance.   —A Course In Miracles

The limited ego will continue based on repeated static or upgraded conditioning. Of course, the natural evolutionary progress of the level of consciousness or clarity of one's awareness will play a role. Within the awakening to Self-realization, an unwavering realization of the natural state of conscious awareness is to some degree complete. Still, the ego/mind continues to play its functional role. But the overshadowing nature of the identification to the individual physical self, the person, and the environment will no longer stick. These attachments will be seen for what they are, the movement of life energy coursing through the individual mind/ body organism expressing activity, just as before, but Consciousness is the dominant motivator. There will also be a period of integration and clearing where Self-realization will expand into new horizons— mainly understanding the mechanics of creation—opening an ever- growing perspective on life's dynamic reality.

From a higher perspective, the ego will respond as it always has in its inherent functionality distinguishing content as appropriated through the sense organs and the organs of action to the conditions of the inner and outer environment. The intellect, through discrimination, will provide context and a relative meaning to the content. The emotions and sensations will respond according to the energetic stimuli presented.

This shift to Self-realization would characterize the normal functioning of the faculties inherent in the mind/body. It resonates with the chakra's subtle energies tied to the nervous and circulatory systems, all organ and brain vitality. On the one hand, the ego is a product of its projected environment. Still, it only comes into harmony with the truth of this fallacy of limited projected conditioning once true awakening or Self-realization has occurred. It is also inaccurate to say that the phenomenal environmental stimuli incite the doing of action. It is one integrated system of the continual movement of self-awareness, knowing itself in all expressed activity that is getting things done. This life force is a source of energy interwoven into the complexity of manifested creation—the glory of living from a unified, Nondual state of consciousness.

> The human being is a self-propelled automaton entirely under the control of external influences. Willful and predetermined though they appear, his actions are governed not from within but from without. He is like a float tossed about by the waves of a turbulent sea, not knowing that he is in the quiet depths of the ocean. Surface waves and floats are

what they are and express the "What Is." The will to action is from the depths of the sea, a mystery, a divine force percolating through the depths as laws and mechanics of nature to the surface to give rise to the multi-various waves of action.

—Nicola Tesla

A quick synopsis: The ego is the mental activity of identification, a function of and for the human brain and nervous system. Ego implies the movement of an actor. The ego ascribes a sense of self within that activity, the **I am**. Ego takes this sense of **I am**, attaches it to the actor, and keeps attaching and claiming ownership. Ego adds. Adding is the reasoning of doer-ship. Enlightenment subtracts. The taking away of a false sense of **I am a body, a thing doing something**. The truth revealed is **I am being lived**.

It seems like at every turn of progress in self-awareness, the ego has crafty and cunning ways to bring back the blanket of identification. This is a chronic function the ego has ingrained over time. The good news is if one hasn't realized true Self, is on the spiritual path, and yet frustrated in recognition that ego is hardened fast to its limited function, there are no worries. Because fighting the ego will only supply it with more energy, who is fighting who? It can only be the ego itself. So, relax into the natural energy flow and just "let it be." Notice its falsehood, the thoughts with the recycling narrative. Notice **I am not the body, not the doer, not the thinker; it is all just happening.** This noticing is one step on the road to recondition habitual patterns.

Let it be as it is and any notion you think or do to be otherwise   —Shivada Amrita

The ego does what it does through the Creators' natural design, and we must give space to that end. Remember, the mistake of the intellect is the culprit in all of this. The intellect is just functioning as it should. It is the mistake of being caught up in material consciousness, the product of this age, the space/time continuum. The level of purity of consciousness expressed in this age is one of low frequency and vibration. It is representative of the current **what is.** We, as spiritual aspirants, rely on what knowledge is available and what works best for us. Simple recognition of this statement frees one to settle into expansion.

> Take what you need and leave the rest behind.
> —The Incredible String Band

Good news also comes from Vedic Knowledge, which goes back millennia and is heralded as the consummate literature cognized by the seers of truth in India. These scriptures transcend modern-day scientific thinking and express practical wisdom to live in peace and harmony. They have simple phrases that outline the human condition, challenges, and place in the universe.

Anoraniyan   Mahato   Mahiyan   (Katha Upanishad,1.2.20)

Atman, finer than the finest, greater than the greatest, is hidden in the hearts of all creatures.

Yatha pinde tatha Brahmande (Purana shloka)

As is the atom, so is the universe; as is the body, so is the Cosmic Body.

Yadvath upari parayana adah (Vedic Shastras)

As above so below, as within so without.

The message from these three ancient passages is that even with our faculties expressing limitations, including all the bodily systems, the ultimate final analysis is an expression of Oneness. The seemingly separate physical structure called the mind/body organism—is Cosmic.

The universal attributes that constitute a human being are the Atman—the Cosmic Mind and Cosmic Body, an individuated reflection of Source energy. "As above so below, as within so without. As is the atom, so is the Universe, as is the body, so is the Cosmic body". These verses point to something that already exists as the Cosmic reality that is all-inclusive. Stunning illumination reveals the ego/mind/body status experienced by sages past and present, pointing to a blessing in disguise. The mind/body organism is and has always been Cosmic. If this is already right here, one can relax knowing everything is well and wisely put from a higher perspective. The realization of **what is** already present is simplified.

Everything becomes valid when one transcends the little ego and becomes the Universal or Cosmic Ego. There is no claiming or identification. Any arising, all arising, whether challenging or benign, are useful expressions or pointers on the journey or progression of consciousness unfolding in higher vibrational dimensionality. Even from limitations, everything is valid. It is just seen from a narrow perspective. It is the essence of the Direct Path to Self-Realization— one that does away with the protracted constant investigation into the nature of enlightenment. One is already enlightened; it is just a matter of remembering.

> Ego is neither positive nor negative; those are simply concepts that create more boundaries. Ego is just ego, and the disaster of it all is that you, as a spiritual seeker, have been conditioned to think of the ego as bad, an enemy, as something to be destroyed. This simply strengthens the ego. In fact, such conclusions arise from the ego itself. Pay no attention to them. Don't go to war with yourself; simply inquire into who you are.
> —Adyashanti

The ignorance and limitations of the 3-D mind are, in effect, functioning as an accelerator tool, if seen properly, to enhance and bring about Self-Realization. This limited state of mind, a form of ignorance, and the projected expressed values that appear in our daily living are none other than a constant reminder to look beyond the ever-changing landscape of the mind. Every action, event, and circumstance holds a clear reflection of your subconscious and the consensus reality you have accepted. For the most part, we miss these signals because we are rolling along nicely, okay by average standards, and not all impressions held in the subconscious are negative or related to trauma. The ones we should intently look at, acknowledge striking false conditioning, should be let go of, and they are buried deep in the subconscious.

Besides, the prime conditioning stems from the **I am the body** idea. It is compelling and accepted without much analysis or inquiry and comes about by an array of very early training and ancestral predispositions. Is this conviction true? And what underlies this false reality that believes **I am someone or something**? It was seemingly handed to us unknowingly on a silver platter, and we have taken it for granted ever since. The power of behavioral conditioning sets up a belief structure so ingrained that it became so common-place and natural. In Nonduality teachings, it is primary to go beyond the **I am**, and to spiritually heal this ingrained conditioned thought, we must transcend it. It is not easy for most people, but one can also work on healing tertiary conditioning that affects our well-being along the spiritual path of transcendence.

If you have heard of Karma and Dharma, it is simply action, activity, and Dharma is the intention according to duty. When the natural movement of Karma/Dharma in one's life is expressed, it is representative of a person's activities or calls to action at any given space/time moment. It represents a Vasana, the Sanskrit term for the Karmic imprint, the memory of any undertaking ever performed. This impression could be benign or challenging, and all experience throughout this life and prior is stored in the subconscious mind as this memory. These stored Vasana's arise from the subconscious as our reality and correspond to any current activity identified by the limited mind. It will show up as a tendency of either grasping or repelling, attachment or aversion. The varying context of a desire, want, or negation of activity is irrelevant to the impetus. Accepting identification for any movement in life naturally occurs for an ego that feels in control. Shying away from any action will be confirmed by the behavioral tendencies exhibited at that moment in time.

The signal to take notice could not be more apparent in the case of distressed emotional impressions, "noticing" is of utmost importance to psychological healing. These latent impressions arising in our day-to-day activity are also called Samskaras. The difference between a Vasana and a Samskara is that a Samskara is the Vasana showing itself from the various mental recollections or memories activating into action from the tendencies inherent in the Vasana. Vasana is the persistent remains of any behavioral trend from a Karmic imprint. The Samskara is the dynamic force behind the Vasana, activating its behavior either externally or internally. Samskaras can lead to more ignorance, or their intention can push the Soul towards the light.

Historically in the wellness camp, mind and body rejuvenation programs have been available since hot baths and the Hippocratic ideal of mental and physical health of the Greeks. To the modern era when Hans Selye in the early 1940s coined the term stress as "the nonspecific response of the body/mind to any demand for change." It brought about the boom in the 50s when the early pioneers in psychology like Sigmund Freud, C.G. Jung, William James, and others brought forward psychological healing through analysis. It is still available today in many styles and forms. Sometimes the results are promising; other times, not so much. It wasn't until the late 60s that yoga meditation arrived mainstream to add a more inner exploration of the mind's capacity to settle and experience peace and well-being. A plethora of adjunct new age healing modalities within a generation had arrived on the scene.

Here we were in 2021, and collective human consciousness continues to struggle despite everything available. One might be tempted to say that science, technology, and medicine are the only way forward to better humanity. Since industrialization, and up to the present, we have seen the good and the massive failings of science, religion, and even spiritual endeavor when dominant political and significant business forces guide hidden agendas.

Hans Selye had it so right; in a nutshell, it is all stress, all psychophysiological movement, from thought to action, all activity from the minor to the significant places a demand for change, or better yet, exhibits stress. From a Nondual-Advaita perspective, our ever-changing experience from a finger pointing to the moon or a huge volcanic eruption is the personal and combined collective space/time realities adjusting to circumstance. Stressors mold reality, "the medium is the message," or "massage," as Marshall McLuhan so aptly phrased it in 1964. The medium and the message are the same; our conscious awareness is experiencing itself as reality molded by our level of consciousness. The medium is your Self, Consciousness. The awareness of something; the focus of your attention is the message. The shape of your reality is equivalent to your state of consciousness.

This is where the disguise comes in when dealing with our reality experience. The entire spectrum of expertise from high blissfully positive to downright traumatic and dark are stressors, the demands for change shaping our reality. Our reality is shaped by our experience, stressors in our inner and outer environment, which are the same. If one has had a bad day, it is a common belief that "I had a stressful day; I need to relax." A good day has also placed a demand or stress on the psychophysiology. The focus or direction for change is neutral, and it is the nonspecific response of any demand on the body/mind that comes in many flavors. In general, the great times we find joy, and in the not-so-great, we would instead put behind us, and the terrible or traumatic the ego buries deep in our subconscious. It is all experience, immanent or in memory, the Karmic imprints, the personal or collective Vasanas and Samskaras that guide our current reality and level of consciousness.

The arising of an event or circumstance, any activity that we do not want to face for whatever reason, is precisely the right time to deal with the present and immediate. Once we realize that any negative Samskaric energy impression can be transmuted into a positive, energetic release, we will have the confidence necessary to face whatever arises from our unconscious. Our fear is simply due to a lack of understanding that immediacy is vital. More so, a recognition that the ego/mind identification is so entrenched in the limited self-perception that the inherent psychophysiological conditioning will continue to repeat as a norm unless we awaken from this false identification. Once we have recognized the importance of present action and the cunning ways of ego, we can, through practice, go beyond the ego and find mental clarity and pacify distorted energies.

The arising Samskara is showing you the way. It is past Karma showing up. You may not want to deal with it, but a message from your guidance arises. Nature's evolutionary force is taking care of you, bringing you what you require. Embrace the energetic vibration of any activity even if it is uncomfortable, feel it into the heart without any judgment or narrative, and watch it dissipate. Breathe deeply, know that you are much more than the arising, breathe deeply into the heart, exhale and relax. All things must pass is a common saying, but those experiences we would like to reject must be recognized fully with immediate intention. Otherwise, those impressions will reshuffle back into the subconscious to be seen another time.

In a benign action tendency arising that holds truth and positive energy, we automatically enjoy its completion. It carries high spiritual energy, but generally, due to ego misidentification and the mind's tendency to label in a way that flatters the ego, we see it as nothing other than a pat on the back. It shows up as a time to savor and reidentify as much as possible. We miss out on the growth implication by getting caught up in the person. These solid positive impressions are indications to further the expansion of conscious awareness, and it is humbling to the self, not personal gratification. You have been gifted to feel the enormity of self apart from the circumstance. It is an opportunity to find the road to peace and contentment and share this reality with others by being your true Self. Evolution is guiding us continually to this all-time reality, the state of enlightenment.

Unresolved negative energy bundles collected and repetitive are part of what ties and grips the ego/mind in contraction. Then it is sometimes easy to fall into this contracted belief and repeat, perhaps unconsciously: "I am suffering. I can't stand this," or "I am to blame for this," or "The environment or someone else caused this." This kind of thinking reinforces the **I am the body** idea and the multitude of other limited material projections. We end up shying away because of uncomfortableness or outright fear, again locking the feelings back into the subconscious. The negative Samskara is necessary to root out for several reasons, notwithstanding the overall effect on overshadowing the mind with suffering, but also psychophysiological health problems arising from these long-standing stressors.

Which is more critical? Clearing these deep-rooted stresses or going after the primary illusion of the **I am the body** idea? It is both; it is simultaneous. They are the same in that one feeds off the other in a seemingly impenetrable loop. They are rooted in and come from a primary belief structure from past ancient human stressors carried through the ages. From our present perspective, our stresses then result from protecting or asserting this separate false self that we have constructed. The severity of identification depends on the individual's particular Karma/Dharma in the evolutionary spiritual journey towards self-realization. It will play out as it will. Some have it relatively easy, and it's just a matter of mild false conditioning and identification by the ego. Others hold deeply seated Vasanas that, in turn, show up as a more solid misidentification with it a lot of unnecessary suffering.

The First Law of Thermodynamics states that energy can neither be created nor destroyed; energy can only be transferred or changed. Natural law exists in our universe, a scientifically proven principle. As human beings, we are all functional in this dimension and express this law in varying frequencies and vibrations defined by our energy bodies, primarily the nervous system and the subtler range of the Chakra and Auric field system. Each chakra emits its unique energy signal vibration. The combined energies of the seven primary chakras form a field around the human body known as an Aura, layered in distinct frequency vibrational fields linked to each chakra. Transforming energy is a natural everyday spiritual occurrence or practice where philosophical belief is not required.

Sadhana or spiritual practice transmutes or modifies energy vibration, discussed in Vedic knowledge and literature. It is the spiritual means to alleviate suffering. Suffering arises and grabs a tight hold on the individual's emotional mind and body. Samskara's need to be seen through for what they indeed are, a conditioned reflex from past action. Once seen and healed, it will not loop back into the subconscious again by taking repeated insight. Sadhana is not exclusively assigned to trials and tribulations of challenging situations only. Everything in life is a Sadhana, part of our spiritual path from birth onwards. Source energy manifested creation to experience Itself fully in many forms and phenomena. Katha Upanishad states: "Atman, finer than the finest, greater than the greatest is hidden in the hearts of all creatures." Source energy wants to experience creation or material value and wants that expression to know itself fully and return home to Source. Sadhana is that journey we call life expressing itself as a Source of energy.

Everything that you have experienced to give rise to this present reality of individual self and what will arise in the future is here as a spiritual guide, a showing to facilitate growth in self-awareness. It may not seem so, but every projected reality you experience within this projected consensus reality of the collective is just a reflection of the inner world that you created. Call it tangible or illusory, form and phenomena. It doesn't matter, but it does express a doorway to lead you back home to yourself. This realization, this lived realization, is the goal of Source knowing Itself through your vehicle.

Universal Ego is a state where all is seen as arising from Universal Will: in the form of no resistance. Karma and Inertia are being played out in the Divine plan. There are no dualities from the absolute level, but right and wrong are essential to level Karma until living that Unified state. From the Universal Ego, the universe is self-organizing and self-correcting. The impetus or movement of consciousness is known to itself fully. Any delusion, although resulting in suffering, is valid because whatever is appearing is our reality as **what is.** Awakening in bliss is the leading light of Reality. Delusion or Maya is the dimension for pure consciousness to have an opportunity to experience and know itself in the bright, shining light of Self.

> This one question, what do I know for certain? It is tremendously powerful. When you look deeply into this question, it actually destroys your whole sense of self, and it is meant to. You come to see that everything you think you know about yourself, everything you think you know about the world, is based on assumptions, beliefs, and opinions— things you believe because you were taught or told that they were true. Until you start to see these false perceptions for what they are, consciousness will be imprisoned within the dream state.
>
> —Adyashanti

The impersonal consciousness of Oneness resonates with each mind/body organism. Driven by ego/mind, the person is experienced as a separate entity outside Oneness. The ego is fundamentally an extension of the Source, but when experienced as distinct, its connection to Source is covered; this is the veil of which Nondual teachings speak. Everything is Source energy, one vast ocean of consciousness, the whole thing, and how could it not be—that is what is meant by Oneness, the premise of Advaita. All differentiated objects manifest from Source retain the whisper identity of illusion that makes them appear physical and as stand-alone objects unto themselves. In appearance only, every atom, molecule, chemical, tissue strand, organ, and surface layer are the vibrating eternal essence of Source manifested. It is the same with ego and all other faculties of the mind. It is all source energy entirely. Of course, mind, ego, intellect, and emotions are not as physically pronounced as the corporeal bodily expression, but they are a subtle material manifestation of Source.

Moreover, the reality is that everything is Source and Source is all there is. Manifest reality has a particular frequency vibration of Source potential that is continuously modified and represented as the evolutionary process. It is easy to come to a confirmation that, yes, this manifest world is Maya. Nothing other than an illusion, abstract thinking that appears and disappears and changes our reality from moment to moment. What exactly are you holding to, the ever-changing that will eventually fade to become the past? Or to something so permanent that its reality is stable, unbounded, and complete? These are the teachings of Advaita, Nonduality. It is within our human capacity to expand this felt sense of being or existence to realize the Oneness, the unity, and actual non-changing value of life.

It is essential to place a caveat to the term "illusion" as used in this context. Advaita nondual teachings describe manifest or material reality as an illusion; a delicate nuance may be missed. From one perspective, this is true, but from a relative perspective, one must be careful not to discount manifestation as illusory totally. It is as natural as the consciousness perspective will allow, even though the relative reality is constantly in flux. The consciousness perspective remains untouched, so to speak, an observer to the observed. Is this observer experienced as unbounded consciousness or some limited expression of awareness? The limited perspective can fall short of ultimate truth reality but still has relative validity and can be called the "reality of illusion." What we are, after all, is what is behind the phenomenal world we ascribe as reality. The truth that upholds any experienced reality is what we are experiencing at any given moment.

Whatever the relative reality perspective is, it can be seen as an illusion because relative reality changes every split second. The past and the future do not exist. There is only your immediate relative perception of the present within the timeless moment of consciousness. However, some experts in consciousness these days would argue, and I would agree that relative reality, whether one wants to classify it as an illusion, is authentic from the "perspective reality" experienced. And why not? It's a Divine expression played out as a living possibility. Is it seen from a limited or an unbounded perspective? Either way and again, the emergence of manifest reality is natural from any perspective. However, the final analysis is an expression of the ultimate Source. Life is reality appearing and living itself as it moves through a sequential presentation. It's as accurate as you believe it is, and it's all valid and reasonable. It also relaxes the mind into a calm acceptance.

> It is false to speak of realization. What is there to realize? The real is as it is always. We are not creating anything new or achieving something which we did not have before. The illustration given in books is this. We dig a well and create a huge pit. We have not created the space in the pit or well. We have just removed the earth which was filling the space there. The space was there then and is also here now. Similarly, we have simply to throw out all the age-long Samskaras which are inside us. When all of them have been given up, the Self will shine alone.
> —Ramana Maharishi

The current scientific investigation points out that the space between atoms and all material objects in the Universe is roughly 100 to 1. There is a lot more nothingness or that unknown energy source than our material creation. And rightly so, if Source is infinite and eternal—and it is challenging to conceptualize, impossible from a material perspective, if you do not live the value of unboundedness. To tap into this, to realize that we are Source, not only as self but as all that exists is the ultimate realization. As Ramana Maharishi says, throw out all the age-long Samskaras inside us and all around us in this reality we perceive. The Self will shine alone then and as it is now.

How does the spiritual aspirant reconcile this recognition of an imaginary world or live it practically in the state of Self-realization? If the seeker is seeking truth, they are also seeking the abiding awareness of the Source and the component potential of energy being activated, which brings about the state of Self-realization. The energy vibrations associated with Self-realization range in exhibited frequency. All conscious perspectives on reality one experiences are modulations of this energy from the Source.

Buddhist teachings speak of a state called Nirvana. A transcendental state where one has gone beyond the personal self. Apparent suffering has ceased, and one is released from the wheel of Karma. It is characterized as a state of non-self, meaning an absolute value of reality has been realized by extinguishing the relative personal domain of existence. But Nirvana is not necessarily or rarely associated with the energy of Ananda where the opening of the Heart, the fourth energy Chakra center, is activated. Nirvana is the realization of Atman, the Soul individuality revealed and referenced from the infinite, unbounded Universal Source. It is complementary to the initial awakening to the Cosmic Self.

The seeker seeking Nirvana, the state without suffering, as a place to escape from Samsara, worldly pleasures, has it all upside down if one feels that the spiritual goal has arrived. A popular misconception in the Buddhist teachings is that one is spiritually complete once absolute reality has dawned, once the self recognizes Bodhi. Seeking may be over, and the attachment to suffering may be over. Yet, if you are present in physical reality and just hiding out in the absolute value, spiritual progress is incomplete.

The world is as you are, but the world is also you as the collective. If you want to enjoy the highest order of Nirvana, you can only do so by continuing to work on the collective engagement of living life. It is accomplished through further refinement of the body/mind organism. Through advanced spiritual techniques involving the group dynamic of awakened individuals, true Enlightenment or Moksha, total liberation within the glory of Shiva/Shakti can be realized. It is when the silence and dynamism, inner and outer realities, are seen as the same Totality.

Sadhana, daily spiritual practice, is seen in every iota of activity from a Self-realized perspective. It is a skill in action when offered and seen from the universal will or the energy of the Source. From a limited mind, it may not carry that type of responsibility. Nevertheless, during this time of extreme energetic polarity, it is necessary to place best spiritual practice forward, to one's comfort level, and live life fully following natural law to whatever degree. Then our peace, contentment, and happiness can be realized in the waking state of this imagined reality. Life is full of vibrating source energy on every level. It's all around us, pervading and permeating every particle. Nirvana is living through the ever-present flow of life, as life, and as an abiding awareness of actual reality. The misidentification of the sticky ego is lessened and finally fully released, and one accepts the status of a Cosmic Ego. Then the real journey begins towards true liberation.

III. NONDOERSHIP AND FREE WILL: THE EVER-SPINNING WHEEL OF KARMA

All there is Oneness: Source. This is the ultimate truth, the highest reality. Phenomenal manifestation arises from this fountainhead of Source energy, and the human being is but one among billions of things. All these objects are part of a vast mechanism, and they function appropriately according to a set of physical laws determined at the onset of creation. And by virtue, we as a species and the whole universe are constantly showing up as our present reality is a testament that the physical laws of nature are supporting the life and longevity of this planet and humankind. It is also true that everything is alive, "the web of life," one breathing wholeness within the container of consciousness. However, the human instrument, as such, does not see its mechanical nature and does not know that it is a machine solely due to the ego/mind. Under the assumed control of the limited ego, its persona sees itself as separate. The world is a playground for manipulation, not realizing the mind/body organism is primarily an object, part of the functioning whole.

The mind and its constituents—ego, intellect, emotions, and sensations, are material manifestations. They function in unison as a processing system on subtle levels of the innermost expression of the human being. Even in its subtlety, the limited mind/ego is still a manifestation of Source and is mechanical in its functioning. The thinking, feeling, and desire interplay as mindset, programming

41

the ego/mind in motion. Specific laws of nature also rule it in a dimension that scientific investigation has not yet fully revealed. Whether mind/ego is functioning through limitations or far more expanded as Atman in a state of Self-realization, physical laws and parameters are set according to one's level of consciousness. One could also call the unbounded mind/ego an integral aspect of the Jiva or the individual Soul.

Therefore, the ego, a faculty of the mind, runs parallel in its energetic material expression, as does the intellect and emotional body. They are of a higher vibration; nevertheless, they are material, a part of physical creation. And material values know nothing other than their set functionality. Although some vibrate at a high level, such as Jiva, your Soul, the expanded Cosmic Mind, there is still a greater reality to unfold towards an integrated wholeness of pure Source.

The mind cannot do or know anything more than its specific function within and as a vibration of consciousness. As an extension of the mind, the ego gives it the reason and process to claim identity through events and circumstances, allowing the intellect to provide meaning to any presented activity. The argument of doer-ship is unequivocal; the sense of ownership of a body and control over occurring action limits the mind's true expression as Cosmic Jiva/Atman. This is the ego; it knows and does nothing else. It is the prescribed software program running since the evolutionary rising of the Sun that gave and gives life.

> The Ego is the imaginary doer behind thought and action. Its presence is firmly believed to be necessary and essential for survival. The reason is that the Ego's primary quality is perception, and as such, it is limited by the paradigm of supposed causality. It is well to keep in mind at all times that the ego/mind does not experience the world but only its own perception of it. —David Hawkins

Individuals will react to whatever is being delivered in the natural flow of life. The variables inherent in the delivery will produce a particular outcome. The outcome is always dependent on the variables of the incoming information energy. If the instrument of the individual receiving the information is not on the same resonance reception level as life's events giving the data, it will be incomplete. It will play a role in response to the energy provided. It all comes down to and is dependent upon the biological and psychological make-up of the individual. This correlation falls short of any proper explanation in the stimulus-response analysis because of the complexity and sheer volume of stored static data in the individual and collective subconscious preceding any action. The world is as you are, and the world you experience mirrors the subconscious self and the collective energies on the planet. There is no way in truly knowing causality, and some Nondual principles point to determinism. Consider it this way, the last domino to fall in a long line of winding dominos, and the domino just behind the last one that falls shouts, I did it, look at me! It's like that.

The principle from the ancient spiritual texts that the "world is as you are" is from the Buddha's *Dhammapada*: "Mind creates the world, what you see arises with your thoughts." Looking from a mundane level, if one is inebriated, then the world will seem topsy-turvy, or if one is high on psychedelics, then the entire perception of the world may be bizarre. These extreme examples show that life's activities or choices impact the recipient's perception of the surrounding environment. Another example is that if someone has had a very stressful day due to a constant flow of activity and cannot keep up, their world will appear hectic and uncontrollable. Still, their co-worker may be calm and collected in the same situation. The same information may have been delivered but with a different response. Why is that?

The truth about all these exterior-interior variables, while they may seem to be evident and plausible from a Nondual perspective, it has been noted that everything, I mean everything, is actually within you. The world is as you are. You project your reality. It reflects your state of Being and is reflected and cast in your mind's eye and perceived as your journey throughout life. With all its ups and downs, glory and sadness—the lot. It is all within your consciousness. The script has been written, the conditioning imparted from birth and added along the way. We have gone through this before, but the key thing to remember is that the script is set. The written script includes this planet with some 8 billion other human beings; the collective consensus reality is intimately related to the reality you perceive. Also, and this is important, one must remember that this reflected reality is more of a guidance system for progress and evolutionary growth in this journey. It is very relaxing to understand that life is life-giving and in our favor 100% of the time.

The script or the software program embedded in your subconscious is mechanical. In truth, it is an electromagnetic signal, but we can say "mechanistic" due to its functionality. The ego identifies this program or script and plays it out as its claim or control of arising content. The ego cannot claim actual **doer-ship** only because of the content with which it is identified; the limited ego's narrow vision misses the context of consciousness as an all-pervading reality. The ego itself is the content.

It's an illusion, a ruse through long-standing conditioning that we, as self-aware beings, fell for so quickly. In the beginning, this awareness of ours was pure, simple, and innocent. It got corrupted by experiencing a space/time continuum point value that resonated more with the low-materialistic frequency vibration than its own high-frequency, which was inevitably numbed down further due to the sheer volume of ignorance present in the world. It was the time we were born into; this was and still present is a period of low vibration. The script has been written.

Consciousness has produced this day. Consciousness
has written the script.

> Consciousness is playing all the characters, and
> consciousness is witnessing the play.
> It's a one-man show   —Ramesh Balsekar

The ego claimed the script's content, falsely claimed **doer-ship**, falsely claimed **I am the body**; following that, it claimed victory. In being the false doer, the ego claimed the product of events, primarily praise for the good and positive ones and shame and guilt for the negative ones. Then it buried the experience in the subconscious, the vast storehouse of impressions as Samskaras, to be released and projected later based on conditioning arising to meet circumstance.

Freedom is impossible if you constantly perceive the body as yourself. The body is part of you, but you are not limited to it. You are the unbounded awareness of consciousness and without limits. It is impossible to fully understand **I am not the body** if one believes one is doing the body's actions. You are not the doer; the feeling of doer-ship is closely tied to the belief that **I am the body**. Whether positive or otherwise, identification with the body's actions will lead to attachment to outcomes. Passions also include nasty ones, such as guilt, shame, anger, and pride. If you are attached and believe you are the body and the doer, these emotional outcomes will be etched in your subconscious and deeply hidden. Your attachment to the experience may have been unpleasant, and you instinctively run away and dismiss negative emotions recycled back into the subconscious.

Being the body is a primordial belief. Actions themselves are the prime validity of the limited ego: you are the doer, and you are the body. It is simply a conditioned belief set through identification from a long time past when the primal ego was in only survival mode— the reptilian mind of flight or fight response. This identification was necessary at that time. Survival of the fittest bode well, not only to stay alive but to carry on the gene pool of the resilient.

Your energy network is distorted by believing that **I am the body and I am separate**. This fundamental imbalance in the holistic energy network places limitations and boundaries on reality. Actions or Karma are seen as different and individual, thus binding oneself to the activities and outcomes. This binding influence of attachments leads to believing that the limited mind and body is the master and not the servant.

> You never identify yourself with the shadow cast by your body, or with its reflection, or with the body you see in a dream or your imagination. Therefore, you should not identify yourself with this living body either. —Adi Shankara

Mind and body are valuable tools meant to be used in navigating life. The purpose of life is not only to live but to live in freedom where the experience of every action is the reflection of source energy moving and exploring itself in the full potentiality of its totality. This Source is inherent in the multivarious expressions that life has to offer. There is no doer of actions; this small "you" that you think you are, is not actually in charge. The limited ego is the belief in the false sense of **personal doer-ship**. Actions just happen. When an actor or the individual doer claims ownership of action, the movement and outcomes are distorted, limited to the 3-D plane of existence. Due to ignorance, it perceives a separate mind or self—this distortion of action when extreme is cut off and redirected to outcomes of either guilt or pride. The shame or pride then refuels the action, becoming even more distorted. One can deny this false ego through simple practices such as meditation and self-inquiry. This false self can also be seen by denying the ego's claim and control over actions.

Dysfunctional behavior develops from the cycle of ignorance and the process of Karma. The false sense of **personal doer-ship** separates you from the universal flow of life and causes actions to become egocentric. When the power of the universal Self is established, the action lands on and through unbounded awareness of self. Then the pure power of life connects to the action, and the universal laws of Nature support the resulting outcome. These universal laws support skillful right action, and the movement produced is needed for that situation. The flow of life is established. **Creative intelligence is the doer** happening through the individual.

The limited mind always expresses reality in dualistic content: experience-experiencer, action-actor. On the contrary, there is no duality. The actor does not experience the action. A closer look will show that the actor is the action. It is all one thing, just *acting*. There is no noun; it's all verbs, only verbs. Perceiving is just happening, and the sense organs and the organs of action are part and parcel of the wholeness of perceiving or experiencing. There is only one thing going on: a *verb,* the movement of awareness or consciousness. It may be arguably stated that there is a perceiver and a perceived, but it's just pure perceiving within one wholeness of Nonduality. Try it on. It's exhilarating and freeing.

We are one with experience. It is just an illusion that we are separate from the experience. No one stands apart from the background and decides to experience the experience: this is key. It is just happening and unfolding as it is, an ever-unfolding moment of now, now, and now. We are lived by it, moved by it, shared by it in the wholeness of the parts. Oneness, God's form as consciousness, is the only experiencer, God's experience of knowing Itself is the "happening."

As humans, we are a materialistic vehicle for this unfolding of glory. All actions are universal actions propagated through Divine power. The Divine spontaneously acts through Nature's laws, which gives rise to this manifest creation. These are the mechanics of creation. Mechanistic as it may be, it is inherently all Divine energy that propels these actions to meet achievement, go onto success, and find fulfillment in Source energy emanating as Divinity. It's a lot to swallow, yet so simple because there is only one thing going on, and you are it. You are **not the body**; you are **not the doer**. It's all misidentification and a projected illusion, a dream, but of course, an incredible dream journey if seen through the eyes of truth or totality.

Suppose you think you are the doer, genuinely a separate individual acting in a world of other independent individuals, all presumable doers, in control of their actions. In that case, you should be able to choose and control your experience. Try to only experience happiness forever. You are in control. Do it; will joy forever, you obviously cannot. Life is just flowing continually in all its variety. It's impressive, a never-ending expression of life living itself. The only time you can say you stop it is when you are in a deep sleep. In a night of deep sleep, we lose the conscious awareness of consciousness. Consciousness is still there but in a pure state, resting as source potentiality. It is a purity of the highest order, unnameable, indescribable, unknowable, beyond all, the mystery.

Free Will: Nonduality and the true nature of the Self

Through investigation, we have seen that you, the person, are **not the doer**; you are **not the body**. Actions occur because our inherent nature is to explore and progress as a species to ever-new horizons. One could say we are following a script that has already been written because wherever you look, there is a constant flow of activity, and it all seems to point in the direction of assumed success. We are all looking for something, a journey's satisfactory conclusion. At the fundamental basis of this energy flow, the creative forces of nature govern all of life. Governing, but not arbitrarily set by a higher power rolling the dice. The higher power is there in the background, and that higher power is you. You represent the energy potential in the form of the universal laws of nature. Before the sequential manifestation of creation, the Atman or Soul individuates from Brahman Source, and the potential inherent individual Dharma/Karma energies expand into lively expression. The human being, its physical and spiritual manifestation, which in truth is one of the highest most precious expressions of Source energy, possesses all these laws or mechanics of Nature within. Through the natural sequential unfoldment of these laws and their interaction, the **Laws of Nature** set up the initial and ongoing script gleaned through the eternal memory of the Veda, the blueprint of creation.

> We see only the script and not the paper on which the script is written. The paper is there, whether the script is on it or not. To those who look upon the script as real, you have to say that it is unreal—an illusion—since it rests upon paper. The wise person looks upon both the paper and the script as one.
> —Ramana Maharishi

From the Veda, not the written literary text about the Vedas, but that level of creation where the potential of Source manifests into energy vibrations and the evolutionary process begins. One could liken them to the possible energy emergence in the Big Bang. These are the Veda, basic eternal laws that govern the forces of evolution, its unfoldment, and the guiding principles behind these expressed laws of nature, which mostly have been uncovered by modern scientific research. Especially in Physics and Quantum Mechanics and the applied Quantum Field Theory. On this level of creation, The Veda, when appreciated fully through conscious Self-realization, the mechanics of creation zoom forth in one's awareness, and we can live the complete knowledge of life's perfection and glory.

> *Richo akshare parme vyoman Yasmin deva adhi vishve nishheheduh* Rig Veda 1.164.39 The origin of the verses of the Veda exists in the collapse of the fullness of Totality, residing in the transcendental field, in which all the impulses of creative intelligence, the laws of nature responsible for the entire manifest creation hum in a state of energetic potential.

Suppose one believes **I am not the body**, and **I am not the doer**, as seen through the lens of Nonduality teachings. Then why does it still feel, even though I am relatively free from the attachments to the outcome, and life seems to unfold as it should, that there still is a strong sense of free will? One has that feeling of free will, and it is more than just a feeling. In the truest sense, it manifests more as choices made during daily activity, such as social interaction, close friends, pursuing education, vocation, and a general outlook on life. Many other personal preferences are simply functional choices made. Life unfolds as it does and continues even after Self-realization. Not many changes on the relative level occur; perhaps some old unsavory habits fall away, and some unexpected new ventures come up and are incorporated, but that feeling of choices being made is always there. The implicit function of the mind/body organism, all the incoming data processing—Sense Perception, the Ego, Intellect, Emotions, and Bodily Sensations remain the same on the relative level. Even with the dawn of a Universal perspective, the sense of free will remains.

However, it all appears to be relative free will, in appearance only, because the person is an illusion, as seen from previous arguments, as is all of creation. A dream being played out by a dream actor. As Self-realization develops or refines in the integration process of embodiment, the more the invention is seen through. But the illusion is not to be discarded; it is a reality from a particular perspective. The dream appearance expresses or manifests through your intimate connection with Creative Intelligence at Source; knowing Itself more deeply through the many expressions within the dream's illusion.

There is no separate person or thing. It's Nondual, not two. Oneness is experiencing itself as Oneness through this apparent multitude of presented objectivity and choices made within the movement of conscious reality. The space between or among all the things or objects is still space as it is. This Oneness of space pervading and permeating manifest creation, unmoved and silent, is the container in which the ever-changing and in-motion material expressions appear.

Closely examining the polarities between Absolute free will and relative free will clarifies more of the relevance for the mind/body from a functional point of view. Absolute free will for a limited ego-based person can not exist. This means there is no small self choosing to do whatever it wants, whenever it wants. Natural selection is governed by natural physical laws inherent in creation. These natural laws limit and guide the expression of free will. The majority consensus reality projected and deemed appropriate within the individual is operational through a conditioned response of the ego/mind. And typically, this response is one of pleasure or pain in reaction to whatever arises. What is often executed is the consciousness paradigm of space and time at any given moment. The choice was apparent in the activity occurring. Still, the free will within the mechanical functioning we call the body/mind organism is a choice made and displayed based on DNA and up-to-date conditioning within the subconscious mind.

The ability to make a free will choice, whatever it is, does not inherently have the full consequences of that action known before execution. If it did, this would be precognition. If we don't see the foreknowledge of any result or ramification of any choice or action, how can we say we could have chosen with absolute free will? The move was seemingly based on a present understanding of the circumstance or situation that seemed to cause the choice to act without fully knowing the outcome.

Absolute free will does not exist because if it did, and foreknowledge of action was known, we could essentially choose based solely on the ever-known outcome. Look at the world around us. It's a hodgepodge expression of passed down inherent genetic heritage and up-to-date conditioning of the individual and collective reality. Freeing your mind is the first step, to release from the ego identification; then free will can be fully realized and seen for what it is, choices made following natural law.

> The question of free will versus predetermination
> is free will versus or against predetermination. You
> consider free will as something you have because of
> the result of a particular thought. But that thought
> occurring, leading you to think it is your free will to
> have, is part of the totality of life functioning. So, it
> is a misconception to consider free will as opposed
> to predetermination.   —Ramesh Balsekar

Relative free will is as much a fantasy as Absolute free will, even though the understanding of Absolute free will is evident in that choices of circumstance such as birth, family, culture, mind/body apparatus are not in our control. There is no absolute autonomy over our inherited experience or prediction of moment-to-moment experience. One seemingly has the choice of day-to-day activity and future planning; however, the outcome is never known. It appears to be relative free will. An appearance only, because from a Nondual reality standpoint, the person is an illusion, as is the entire creation. As said before, the appearance of reality is mechanistic in function, projected by the mind. The nature/nurture of evolutionary forces ever modifying the apparent individual and world is also mechanical. It is all a formulation of the mechanics of natural law or God's realization of creation, which is expressive of Source energy. Universal intention and individual intention are seeds planted within the potentiality of all possibilities. Deeds are done, but there is no personal doer. Free will, absolute or relative within the Advaita doctrine, coincides with determinism/predeterminism. Contemporary Nondual interpretation has it more from an individual biological determinism of genetics and life conditioning set forth by the immutable laws of nature. And the level of clarity in one's consciousness determines one's perspective of reality.

That ever-persistent **I-ness** gives the natural feeling of having free will; call it absolute or relative, it does not matter. Whatever way you analyze or synthesize the exploration, **I-ness** is always there, within the ignorant or enlightened. We are not talking about the feeling **I am**, which was exposed as a sham long ago when the ego/mind was seen as a machine. It is the **I-ness** that transcends, if you will, all the way to the precept of existence. Explaining existence and the ever phantom **I-ness**, the actual reality of **I** the awareness, with words, will never do it justice. You can only point to it, or better yet, be it. It's a thread, an intrinsic self-realized connection through expanding consciousness. Hold that to be the truth, the unchanging Self.

The sense of individual free will is valid on one level. It has its origin in energetic reality and truth. Still, it is a feeling only because it is the free, unbounded will of Source energy that we pick up on through the intimate connection with the Source and the existence of the Self. This connection is the same pure consciousness curving back on itself and becoming conscious of itself as awareness. It is the simple initial act of creation manifesting at the most refined expressed level. Source potential in its movement is Universal Will, knowing itself as the creative power of pure consciousness. Intelligence and joy are expressed in exploring its potential as Source eternal through continued, repeated re-creation of itself. In essence, we are that, and what we as an individual pick up on is the willpower of God the Creator, or Source energy manifesting its potentiality. It is this thread of sublime energy which unites us.

If you are **not the doer** and **not the body**, and everything is just arising based on ancestral DNA and up-to-date conditioning, then any notion of free will is just the surfacing of the illusion; it's a dream within the dream character. How can it possibly have free will outside of its conception of the dream? It is just a feeling of free will, sensed and picked up on from the freedom and willpower of the Universal Self, enjoying and creating the play of life. Recognition of this highest freedom of will by an individual is decisive and empowering.

> When you get out of the driver's seat, you find that
> life can drive itself, that actual life has always been
> driving itself. When you get out of the driver's seat,
> it can drive itself much easier; it can flow in ways
> you never imagined. Life becomes magical. The
> illusion of the "me" is no longer in the way.
>
> —Adyashanti

A personal me doesn't become free; they can't, they are an illusion, and an illusion is incapable of Moksha, freedom, or ultimate liberation. You become free of the "me" in this apparent reality when you have realized the unbounded Self-awareness that has always been present—the Source potential manifest at inception, containing all that there is, all that will ever be. The script has been written, and nothing is new under the Sun. The light of pure consciousness, the Oneness of Being.

> All the activities the body performs are
> predetermined. The only freedom you have is
> choosing not to identify with the body performing
> the action.   —H. W. L. Poonja

Karma Yoga, the union of action, the whole seeing of the dynamics of activities, is the back door entrance into Nonduality when you see it through a **non-doer ship**. Ask yourself, "Am I doing the action, or am I observing the activity?" Choose the one that feels more accurate. You cannot make an effort without watching it. There is a place in you that is the witness. It is the place of a sense of being or existence. A place before thought. A place we call presence, a presence or abiding awareness that is devoid of the separate self. We all know of this presence, to some degree or another. Just like the sense of gravity that we experience and know exists as a mysterious force of nature throughout the cosmos. What is this force doing by holding everything together and apart? What do you suppose is behind this sublime force? The closer you get to an answer, the closer you are to the Source. And the closer you are, the more paradoxical it appears to be, together and apart. How does gravity even do that? The paradox is the staple of Nondual/Advaita philosophy teachings, as is all of creation if one lives in the Quantum Reality. There is something even more subtle uniting all paradoxes, and that is the intelligence behind existence, the same sense of presence you can tap into easily. It is the natural you, undefinable, unbounded Source. Intelligence with an **I** concealed within the mystery of itself beyond imagination.

IV. PAIN AND PLEASURE; SUFFERING OR NOT, THE MECHANICS OF IGNORANCE, THE KARMIC TRAP

The carrying of stress in our human organism, stored physically and emotionally in the energy nervous system, does not have much of a chance of alleviating, as one is constantly motivated to move forward. Believing that one must accomplish, make things happen, succeed in life, coupling that belief that we are responsible for our actions under our power. We experience guilt and shame, pride and prejudice when activities performed are not fulfilled, or in the case of some achievement, it will be internalized as momentary success at best. The result of unfulfilled actions that lead to feelings of guilt, shame, or blame for the limited mind feeds and strengthens the ego to recycle these actions and keep us in bondage through a false sense of control.

> Your worst enemy cannot harm you as much as your own unguarded thoughts. Develop the mind of equilibrium. You will always be getting praise and blame, but do not let either affect the poise of the mind: follow the calmness, the absence of pride.
> —Gautama Buddha

All that we are is the result of what we have thought. The Mind is the keeper of everything. We are not

> responding fully to this moment if we are judging
> any aspect of it. The mind is everything, what we
> think we become.   —Maharishi Mahesh Yogi

The ego-self or conscious mind is the facilitator, and the subconscious mind is the storehouse of memories. From the limited perspective of ego/mind, the self appears to control individual actions. The conscious mind and sub-conscious operate in tandem, but the reality is not seen for what it truly represents from a limited ego perspective. Reality is the subjective observer, and the ego operating as a mechanical function sees reality only as objective and separate. The subconscious holds the Karmic impressions of one's entire lifetimes on profound energetic levels. The subconscious or higher self wants nothing more than to reconcile the Karmic imprints and free itself from the ego's delusion to enjoy Universal status. The relentless cycle of ego projection of unreality contributes to and perpetuates ignorance and evolutionary stagnation, binding one to the wheel of Karma and its identification. It is challenging to get off this loop that the ego/mind habitually recycles, and the misidentification with material reality is involuntary.

> The attachment to beliefs is the greatest shackle. To
> be free is to know that one does not know.
> —Wu Hsin

Relativity, the illusory manifest world, is as vast as the infinite; the only distinction is bound by a time/space continuum of limitations. Lost in this seemingly vast universe and complexity of life, the human being is unaware of how utterly simple living life is. This book intends to bring awareness or shine clarity in the individual's mind about the dynamics of consciousness and the mechanics of the natural flow of reality. This personal world we engage in is but an extension of our pure awareness for the sole purpose of coming back home, realizing the self as the unity of Oneness.

In the ancient tradition of Vedic India, it was customary for the children's first fourteen years to be deeply involved with spiritual knowledge alongside the practical life application. From an early age, cultivating spiritual awareness was a prime stepping stone to engaging in life confidently and fully.

We are here, obviously, and we are doing what we do and, for the most part, hoping for the best or even a better outcome. Living and loving, we value goodness and ease, happiness and contentment, goodwill, and self-acceptance as hallmarks of a successful life. We desire a sense of satisfaction at the end of life. The funny thing is the end of life is always and hopefully far in the distance. The end of life is not something we entertain too often. We keep pushing forward without the slightest notion of why, what, and where all this activity will end. We rationalize the purpose of our human condition with great answers or even simple affirmations to help soothe the road we are on. We are blind, totally ignorant of the actual status and glory of ourselves and life.

We are caught in what many nondual teachers classify as the Spirit—Mind—Body complex. That is a good model. Jesus had it right; Father, Son, and Holy Spirit. This trinity, seen in many other spiritual cultures and religions, represents three primary energy dimensions that govern life. It's beautiful, the Holy Spirit as Source energy, Father as God the creator, and Son or Christ as manifest creation. The Vedic tradition is slightly different in that they encapsulate the Father's value as the triumvirate personified as Gods Brahma, Vishnu, and Shiva. Brahma is the creator aspect, Vishnu, the maintainer aspect, and Shiva the aspect of dissolution. Brahman, another term from the Vedas, is the ultimate Universal Reality, the three-in-one structure of Unity. In some sense, this could be equated as Source or Spirit energy. And the Atman individuated Brahman is representative of human or the worldly creation, the Christ value. So, both traditions present a Trilogy of primal energy emanating from the Source to structure the levels of manifest creation.

From a Nondual perspective, Spirit would be the infinite energy, pure consciousness, and cannot know itself without a mind. Spirit is just the **Is-ness**, and it can be equated with **I-ness**, the invisible initial intent of Brahman, and this is where language falls short, and semantics takes over. Brahman describes nothingness when lived through the human nervous system as gradations of the vacuum. The emergence of **I-ness**, that infinite energy of pure consciousness, is a dimensional state integral for human evolution and the spiritual journey to the fullness of the Self-liberated state. It cannot know itself without a mind.

The second component of the Spirit/Mind/Body Complex is the mind. It is the tool or mechanism of reflection for emotions, sensations, and thought. It also has faculties of ego and intellect to give the mind the ability to localize awareness to a point value in space and time. In turn, the mind can't know itself as a phenomenon without a physical body, the brain and nervous system, and all energy fields and centers comprising the form or function.

The last and third component is the body. Why does the mind require the body to know itself, and the Spirit or Brahman needs the mind to know itself? It is one complex integrated system of parts. Parts work in unison to deliver a sum value significant of wholeness, the reality of Brahman. The internal and external fullness of life. Plain and simple, we are on an evolutionary journey, and we are reaching for the Ultimate Reality of Truth to dawn and become an all-time reality. It will take all parts known and unknown to function in dynamic synergy to bring about that highest frequency vibration of Truth. However mundane and illusory it may appear, the body is vital in this dream world unfolding. It plays its role in the script that has been written in the Veda, the blueprint of creation.

When dealing with the mind, body, and spirit relative to the mechanics of ignorance, the veil covering the true self, it is crucial to explain how pain and suffering arise and what knowledge one can gain from this energy dimension. First, remember the mind in its ultimate truth is Cosmic. It extends as far as manifest reality does infinitely. The concept of unboundedness and infinity is challenging to grasp unless you live it, and still, from that level, what may be described is immediately limiting.

However, one can easily imagine the vast material universe to whatever extent and picture the ever-expanding cosmos. The entirety of manifest creation has some ring to it, but imagine there is no end to it, ever, no limitations from a 3-D perspective. With this magnificent enormity in mind, briefly take in the totality it represents, and that totality defined as Brahman is the essence of eternal Infinity.

What it also means and so contained are expressions of the personal consciousness: the Atman, the Jiva/Soul, the mind, the ego, the intellect, and emotions in that they are integral to the individuation of Self, the Cosmic Self or universal **I-sense** from Brahman, the attribute-less source totality.

The body is the most outer physical expression of ourselves. Physiology is a microcosm of the universe. The diverse laws of nature that create and maintain the vast, ever-expanding universe are found on every level of human physiology. The cell and the DNA are at the core of our psychophysiology. The various systems that make up the functional body apparatus are expressed in packets of energy frequency on the subtlest level within the genome and cellular structure. It is akin to and described on the quantum field level of the human body, the unified field of everything. These packets of energy or quanta are virtually existent but mathematically verified as physical reality. Beyond that and pervading everything is the unmanifest potential of creation. Resting there, straddling both manifest and unmanifest reality, on the level of the human body are the repercussions of consciousness, the immutable laws of creation. At the quantum level of reality, this portal is the genesis of our structured human physicality. In essence, on that level, the Body can also be seen as Cosmic, one integrated wholeness. An expression of the Unified Field.

Navo-Navo bhavati jayamanah Rig Veda 10.85.19
In the process of transformation or evolution,
Totality is reborn again and again.

The totality of consciousness is held in every point
value of creation. Seeing totality at every point
means seeing it in quanta, an elementary particle
or atom, a molecule, a cell, or organ, or in a human
being. Even the planet Earth can be considered as
a point value.   —Maharishi Mahesh Yogi

The mind in its Cosmic reality as Atman, which is individuated
Brahman, is the totality, and that totality is you as wholeness. It is
located within the most delicate value of Mind, the Veda, and the
Akashic Field, the memory imprinted in your subconscious. There
is the memory of Brahman, the universal self, and the memory of
Atman, the personal self. When perceiving the world, all you are
projecting are those memories to be picked up by your five sense
organs, processed, and reflected onto the screen of life. Depending
on your state of consciousness, the reflection varies from a limited
perspective to an expanded one. "The world is as you are." And in
the final analysis, whatever the view, you have always been that
Cosmic reality, full stop.

Nothing perceived is independent of perception,
and perception differs not from the perceiver,
therefore the universe is nothing but the perceiver.
                    —Abinavagupta

"You are what you see; you become what you see" is a popular
saying of Maharishi Mahesh Yogi. You are bombarded by bits of
sensory impulses every moment. Most are filtered out selectively
and automatically by your conscious and subconscious mind. What
you allow into your awareness, and it's a tiny fraction, is directly

determined by your habitual patterns of interpreting the world set in place by the Karmic impressions carried in your subconscious. It is a fanciful loop of memory from the earliest time in the chain of individuality. These Samskaras, individual and collective, run our lives, and the ego/mind thinks it is running the show. See the false. See what is unreal within your mind.

The individual mind in ignorance represents only a tiny percentage of its wholeness. This small part of the full potential carries over as the personal ego and the primary default perspective of separation. The ego identifies mind, body, and the sense of inner spirit as separate and distinct from one another. Separation leads to fear, and fear is the natural consequence of comparative values expressed by a limited analyzing mind using the stunted power of its intellect or discriminating faculty. The ego isn't to blame; it organizes experience to give meaning to the manifest creation. It's only from the platform of limitation that the ego runs wildly, causing the non-supportive energy and the misidentification of Karma or activities arising to the individual mind/body.

Guilt and pride are the primary weapons of the ego to keep us in a state of spiritual sickness and toxicity. Using the coin analogy, guilt and pride are two seemingly separate sides, but they are the same in a higher reality. From the perspective of the subconscious mind, it is all neutral; it does not distinguish between real or not real, between good or bad, everything is valid. Guilt and pride arise and have distinct energy signals. The corresponding feeling is definitive when the ego appreciates any arising emotional energy. But initially stored latent in the subconscious, the energy signal is neutral on that level.

So, whenever the conscious mind or limited ego labels the results or outcome of life's day-to-day journey in experience, it does so with the automated intent to shame or blame through guilt or to self-indulge with a narcissistic pat on the back to the small self through pride. Guilt and pride harbor this sickness simply through identification and misinterpretation from long past conditioning, through either appropriate action or non-life supportive action, that have been buried in the subconscious mind, the storehouse of all impressions.

When one awakes from a deep sleep in the morning, consciousness comes online, and the first thought, and it occurs lightning-fast, is **I am the body**. From there, a flood of subconscious impressions of what it means to the mind/ego to presently be the body is reflected into the environment as energy frequency vibrations in multitude. The senses pick up these electro-magnetic energy signals, process them through the nervous system, and flash the vibratory signal patterns onto the brain's occipital lobe. Neurons firing throughout the brain and nervous system are then collated on the 3-D screen of the Mind and projected as information in our seen reality. It is accomplished in milliseconds. How marvelous is this human mind/body organism structured by Universal natural laws and the force of Creative Intelligence? We take this for granted and are also held captive by its mechanics. We are unaware of consciousness's total potential and reality.

> When somebody or something provokes your anger, the only reason you get angry is that you're holding on to how you think something is supposed to be. You deny the 'What Is.' Then you see it's the expectations of your Mind that are creating your own hell. When you get frustrated because something isn't the way you thought it would be, examine the way you thought, not just the thing that frustrates you. You'll see that a lot of your emotional suffering is created by your models of how you think the universe should be and your inability to allow it to be as it is.
>
> —Ram Dass

Similar life moment arising from the projected mind/ego when seen, processed by the subconscious, and reflected as verifiable content is a means to naturally move forward in life from any perspective of consciousness that one might have. The reality unfolding is reputable, a repeatable guiding principle to be fully aware of what that seeing represents. Still, it is unfortunately hijacked by the limited ego where false conditioning is projected instead.

Therein lies the loop, or the wheel of Karma, from an immediate experiential perspective. The misidentification of that moment-to-moment experience relates to similar energy signals stored as impressions in the subconscious. It triggers the effect or meaning. Then the inevitable labeling of the conscious ego/mind on a visceral, energetic level that substantiates the memory. Whatever it may be, pain or pleasure, immediately burying the negative experience back into the subconscious if a painful response is initiated. A positive experience can repeatedly languish as the energy of pride takes over, rewashing the ego and imprinting the experience back into the subconscious.

This imaginary non-truthful mechanical response by the limited mind/ego is behind any experience in life when seen through false up-to-date conditioning. But the hidden gem in consciousness is that one can break this loop of ignorance by self-investigation through direct seeing and experience. Your conscious awareness is the same consciousness inherent in the world around you; meditation practices and familiarity with the teachings of self-inquiry will expose awareness as the primary lead to a higher reality of existence. Diminishing that sense of separateness into an integrated consciousness reveals there is only one consciousness, and you are it. That Oneness is a reciprocal flow of Universal or God's love in the display of dreamer and the dreamed. The dream continues but is seen for what it truly is, the exploration of consciousness. How does one aspire to or even get to this idyllic recognition of Self-actualization?

The first step is through acute self-investigation, the intellectual recognition provided by teachings of Nonduality. The instructions of Nondualism extract and point to the mechanical nature of manifest creation; they reveal the character inherent in the mind/

body organism and its relationship within the universal trilogy of the Spirit/Mind /Body complex. Re-structuring the conditioned belief system revealed and appropriated through understanding the principles of Nonduality.

The second step is direct experience of Self through meditation and culturing the silence of unbounded consciousness. Repetition is the mother of invention—re-condition the old, long-standing inappropriate beliefs by seeing a new perspective repeatedly through different angles of approach. The awareness of Self develops a greater appreciation for the laws of nature guiding all of creation. We can tangibly experience the progressive expansion of consciousness and validate our growth through ancient scriptures and modern scientific knowledge.

All these seemingly intricate mechanics and dynamics of the parts within the wholeness of consciousness are just that, parts. From the overview that there is only one thing going on, and that is Oneness expressing the many in the unconditional flow of life, it is quite simple to relax and find confidence knowing the teachings of Nonduality are from an ancient lineage expounding eternal truth. However, even though the reality of Self can be revealed by stripping away the veil of ignorance, it will still be experienced as a process—an experience based on repetition and re-conditioning the mind. The more you place your attention on something, the more it flowers.

> Even after the truth has been realized, there remains that strong, obstinate impression that one is still ego, the agent, and the experiencer. This must be carefully removed by living in a state of constant identification with the supreme Nondual Self. Full awakening is the eventual ceasing of all the mental impressions of being an ego.   —Adi Shankara

The statement of Oneness is still conceptual. It is difficult for the intellect to digest fully and discern whatever Oneness represents.

It's the coin spinning at high velocity with the **I-ness** on one side and **Is-ness** on the other. The **Is-ness** is the sense of being, existence, and **I-ness** as the unknown mystery, Source energy. They are in one sense the same because, at that level of quantum reality, unification is supreme. The coin evokes no differentiation, no distinction, just complete gratitude and surrender to the benevolence of Wholeness, the holiness of Oneness. What would cause an emotional feeling of the joy of truth behind this sense of Oneness? It is the activation of the Heart Chakra, the unifying value or principle within the energy signature of Love. Let your heart open to whatever that high-velocity spinning orb representing the Cosmos means to you. The feeling will evoke the intimate core of existence. And you are that.

I am That.—Nisargadatta Maharaj.

One can undertake various practices with insight into these mechanics of ego/mind used to clear the deep-rooted conditioning that causes intolerable pain and suffering. It all starts with pain and pleasure. We will always experience pain and joy as we navigate life. These two will seem to run your life; they are an unavoidable part of the human condition. These two primordial energy outcomes arise from any experience we have as we progress through life.

And this makes life worth living from the relative perspective, in the excitement of an unknown activity just around the corner waiting to be experienced. Although still unavoidable and written into the script of life, the signature of an energetic vibratory effect arises. Painful or pleasurable, tied directly to any Samskara imprinted in our subconscious, and either one, in essence, is pure consciousness. Whatever is experienced, whether pain or joy, does not lead to suffering. Suffering is just the continued identification by the limited ego to an invalid interpretation of the arising Samskara impression from memory.

> Between the banks of pain and pleasure, the river of
> life flows. It is only when the mind refuses to flow
> with life and gets stuck at the banks that it becomes
> a problem. By flowing with life, I mean acceptance,
> letting come what comes and go what goes. Desire
> not, observe the actual, as and when it happens,
> for you are not what happens; you are to whom it
> happens. —Nisargadatta Maharaj

As challenging as pain is, as it is with pleasure, it arises as a conditioned response to circumstance. We have no idea what will be next and what will follow. One can mitigate pain, psychological or physical, by becoming resilient as a human being as much as possible through implementing a health and wellness regimen. It is essential to strengthen the psychophysiology to lessen the impact of pain. But it will arise nevertheless, and if one recognizes the mechanics surrounding the experience of pain, then regardless of the severity, one does not have to suffer from it deeply.

Suffering is caused by the loss of conscious awareness by the ego's identification of the experience outcome, in this case, negative energy. From a relative level, negative energy can be mitigated in several ways, seeing it for what it is and represents, and adding healing modalities, psychological or physical, either through mainstream therapies or metaphysical energy healing techniques. It's all available, but the first thing is seeing what and why of any pain arising, which means facing it. It is not necessary to recap the story but to engage fully with the feelings behind the story.

Many healing modalities release the energy signature representing the specific trauma or pain. They are all available from ancient to modern cultural techniques, the metaphysical to scientific. Some work well, others not so. No one likes pain, with very few exceptions, but that in itself is a massive trauma. Pain and suffering go hand in hand if not taken care of; true healing comes with spiritual awareness, cleansing the soul to appreciate its unbounded Divine status. Given our current planetary situation, man's relative pain is inevitable, but one does not have to suffer the Karmic consequence of pain.

> When we start to suffer, it tells us something very valuable. It means that we are not seeing the truth, and we are not relating from the truth. It's a beautiful pointer. It never fails. —Adyashanti

Pleasure is positive energy, but it is also transitory, as is any experience. It is not an abiding truth because it will always dissipate. What's next? Will it come back, or might it be more pleasurable? If pleasures arise, then yes, enjoy the experience and feeling, but it is important to recognize that pleasure will cease on its own, so let it go. Hanging on to it, constantly looking for the same experience or facsimile, becomes suffering in itself. Expectation to an outcome, attachment to something not realized, is all suffering, and in the most intense degree, it manifests as an addiction.

> The tragedy of an attachment is that if its object is not attained, it causes unhappiness. But if it is attained, it does not cause happiness; it merely causes a flash of pleasure followed by weariness, and it is always accompanied, of course, by the anxiety that you may lose the object you were looking for.
> —Anthony de Mello

One must let go of any experience; it's just an experience. Don't allow the ego to wrap it up in an identity, where one shelters activity in avoidance of pain and where one has so identified with pleasure that it becomes an obsession. These things happen on their own based on your up-to-date conditioning and DNA/genetic coding. Experiences lead to more adventures. It is one fluid motion of experiencing that's living life. Yes, there are lessons in each incident, but the bottom line is they are all clouds, some beautiful and some dark, all passing over the landscape of the sunlight of Self-awareness. Accept each experience fully and what it has to offer. Take care of the painful ones in the best way possible, savor the pleasurable ones as long as they last and be mindful of the ego's tendency to elaborate a story about the event.

The stored memory of deep-rooted pain and trauma caused by psychological or physical events are the same. The energy signature is locked on both levels, which is partly the makeup of the total energies of the subconscious. The mind will re-enforce that idea or memory because that is what the mind does, it gives meaning and identity to experience, and all experiences are valid on the level of the subconscious mind. Stored in your subconscious, they are neutral latent impressions or memories of an incident. When catalyzed by an environmental trigger, the behavioral or mental images of a traumatic experience may re-surface in one's mind. Reliving a traumatic experience may be frightening. The impulse is to run and hide. This is ego in all its color, totally overshadowing one's Awareness.

Suffering is the Ego's loop to recycle the hardened notion of separation. It works very well. You are either suffering or afraid of suffering, keeping the individual locked into the limited mind/body organism, the physicality of suffering being a reality. Pain will occur in life, but suffering does not have to follow. We suffer because of the profoundly ingrained energetic imprints stored in the subconscious over many lifetimes that continue to resurface and the ego's identification and inability to see past this imaginary veil. The deeper and heavier the marks, the more the ego narrates an exclusive storyline, and we suffer believing the story. As long as the ego recycles these impressions, we will never free these habitual energy patterns. By closely examining the mechanics of these patterns and bondage and recognizing the ego's role in this process, we can begin to loosen the knots of Karma.

The subtlety of stored imprints as Samskaras may be apparent, considering we are dealing with the level of energy. Still, these energy signatures are contained within and surround the mind/body organism in the subtle body's dimensional realms. The subtle bodies of the human being are representative of the connection between the physical and spiritual realities. It generally comprises and is seen as the surrounding Auric field extending from the human body. They are the Physical-Etheric body and the Emotional and Mental bodies of denser energies, then into a higher frequency vibration the Astral body plane, the connection to the spiritual realm.

Further and more refined in frequency, the Celestial body is a blueprint for physical existence within the spiritual plane. It is then followed by the Causal Body and the Transcendental Cosmic/Divine body, both of a higher order. The Causal body or Soul contains the volitional impulses of Vasanas. And the Samskaras, the energetic projection of any notion within the Vasana, permeates all subtle body realms below Divinity. Life's experiences imprinted as memory are all part of and stored in the subconscious, but the overall consciousness is the container of these subtle body realms. To fully realize the extent of Enlightenment or Moksha, the total liberation of self, then focus on expanding self-awareness, one's attention must be applied to release and heal these impressions on all subtle body energetic levels.

V. SPIRITUAL MODALITIES TO EXPAND CONSCIOUSNESS AND TO HEAL THE MIND/BODY ORGANISM

There are three ways of describing the journey to awakened consciousness in the Nondual theatre. While the approach towards a state of liberation free from the limited ego/mind's apparent control may vary, the resulting realization of spiritual freedom is a perspective of Oneness. There is only Oneness, but the degrees of freedom within Oneness, your perspective reality, depends on one's awakened consciousness level.

1. An ardent discipline and practice characterize one's journey to spiritual freedom. Meditation and Self-Inquiry contemplation are incorporated into a routine to realize one's essential nature or higher Self. Spiritual growth towards Nonduality is achieved through this journey where one may feel or seem to be on a "path." This practice gives one a feeling of tangible accomplishment, community, and shared experience. Daily eyes closed meditation methods may vary significantly. The contemplative self-inquiry approaches are similar in that investigation may go to the heart of exposing the self or rely on reconditioning belief structures.

2. Another approach to Nondual recognition is more of a direct path where, when involved, the term path is not favored because of natural means already here and present.

The pathless path, crossing through the gateless gate. It is accomplished by seeing through the limited self through focused awareness or applied attention. It is habituating or reconditioning the mind and belief structure. It runs parallel to all the Mindfulness techniques available today, noticing the presence, the now. The direct path to Nonduality requires self-honesty and effortless focus, which involves mastering the ability to *"Look and Be"* within a collected awareness.

3. The third path is viewed as absolutely no "path." There is nothing to do, nothing that can be done. It is radical Nonduality where there is no small self and never was, only Absolute Oneness. This realization has absolute validity, but it is not the whole eternal Truth. There is the total value, the no-thing-ness of Source infinite, which is your most authentic Self, and relative existence is but a whispered illusion; but what is the point in only honoring the absolute value? If one is embodied in the realization of absolute reality, then hanging onto or getting lost in the notion of nothingness is not living the whole truth of embodiment. The Nondual reality from the fundamental perspective is unknowable by a person, but if you are living through this body as Absolute reality, then do so entirely as Source Reality intended—the nature of Awakened Self blossoms with all its relative qualities of Love, Compassion, and Wisdom.

The messages are identical in recognizing that the separate self is not authentic; our true Self is only a timeless, infinite reality of Oneness. We can integrate all three so-called paths, emphasizing the first one, which aligns with the knowledge gained through direct experience of Samadhi meditation, and then contemplative understanding of that experience through Self-Inquiry to realize the illusory nature of the small self. The Nondual reality, from its origins, as espoused by Adi Shankara, has both these components of knowledge and experience together as verification of realized existence. Adi Shankara also emphasizes Vedic Knowledge where at its Source, the primary qualities of Oneness expressed are Sat—Chit—Ananda. The Purity, Intelligence, and Blissful Nature of the Self, respectively. When adopting a Nondual journey to self-realization, it is essential to understand that Oneness is not static, inert, or dry; it is the Wholeness of parts that all inherently contain Sat Chit Ananda as the core qualities.

Meditation Techniques

There are lineages of spiritual ascension throughout recorded history and presumably beyond. There are a wide variety of spiritual practices available today which are being explored and verified through a modern scientific approach. Many methods of meditation are very similar, and there is much crossover. Still, it comes down to four process styles: Effortless, Contemplation, Concentration, and lastly, a compilation of any preceding methods done through a Guided or Group Meditation setting.

1. Effortless meditation uses the mind's natural tendency to search for more happiness, which it finds in achievement and fulfillment through thought and action. The nature of the mind runs parallel to the force or progress of evolution. More and more forward towards expansion. Our minds are habituated to look or search outwardly for this happiness. As we have seen, repeated simple conditioning from birth makes it necessary to learn a correct practice to spontaneously alter the mind's habitual outward tendency and direct itself inward.

It is difficult, sometimes seemingly impossible, to direct the mind in meditation inwardly to explore the depths of the mind and arrive at the reality of the Source. The conditioned mind always looking outward for completion is a hardened habit over centuries and requires a little help, a technique to guide it inwards. Effortless meditation also uses vehicles to dive into the depths of the mind—breath, sounds, phrases, mental concepts, and, of course, mantras.

In the Vedic tradition and heritage of gaining Knowledge, or Self-realization of Source, it is understood that the material world and everything in it is that Source, the only Source in you, me, and all that there is. At the level of Sat Chit Ananda, those initial qualities of Source expressed also underlie and permeate all. Primarily Chit or the Intelligence factor is hidden as the creative impulse in the blueprint of creation, the Veda, hence the Vedic Knowledge. The Veda has a three-in-one structure, and on that most refined level of inception, all three characteristics are at homogeneous stasis. The Shruti: energy sound vibration, Smriti: memory field of all possibilities, and Purananam: the-all, ancient, pure origin. In the Veda, there hums the sounds of the Veda, the Shruti aspect of Source potential, the sounds, frequency vibrations that arise to become form and function of the phenomenal world. These sounds in Vedic terms are known loosely as Mantra.

These mantras have a specificity unto themselves and are the blueprint of creation right from the Source to the surface value of Reality. Vedic Knowledge identifies these sounds and the form produced as cognized by the seers of reality and passed down orally or written in scripture. These sounds eternally humming at inception within and at the doorstep of Source express their form and function thoroughly at that supreme fine level, providing them with immense power. The sounds, Mantras are utilized as vehicles to meditate. They facilitate an effortless deep dive of mind, gravitating towards energetic dimensionality where the sound hums at its origin.

The mind inherently, as said, has a natural tendency to seek higher energy stimulation and happiness. These inner levels of the mind contain these higher energetic levels. It's like drawing a parallel to physical reality through quantum physics where it is a fact that the more refined, or subtle, the field of inquiry, the greater is the inherent energy power. Without the slightest effort from the individual in the practice of mantra meditation, the mind's tendency will automatically dive within on the coattails of the specific mantra. Effortless it is, but an initial condition of instruction must be set, a bit of direction to consciousness, so the mind takes the correct angle into that effortless dive. We incorporate and promote this kind of meditation in our Nondual teachings and Self-realization platform because it provides a pure and direct experience of Source energy or that state of no thought. This experience is none other than the true Self.

Vedic Knowledge is the direct experience of knowing the Truth of life coupled with intellectual understanding. These are the mechanics of nature in the evolution of the spiritual journey. This knowledge comes from a long lineage of realized masters predating even Adi Shankara, who established the four seats of knowledge in India and later became known as Shankaracharya. Experts in Shankara's teaching were meant to preserve this knowledge in its purity and pass it down from master to ready disciple. One of the last and most venerable of the Shankaracharya was His Divinity Brahmananda Saraswati of Jyotir Math (1871-1953). He presided over the northern seat of Shankara's established four seats of knowledge in India. He was also known as Guru Dev, who passed this timeless knowledge to his beloved disciple Maharishi Mahesh Yogi, who then was compelled to share it with the world as the Transcendental Meditation program.

2. The second type of meditation is contemplation. Sitting on the serene banks of a river flowing with ripples, tides, and eddies, a person may quietly merge with the sounds and sights of nature, as natural and complete in its quality of expanse as the stillness within. It is the same feeling as one contemplates the heart of the self. **Who am I?** What is the actual reality of self, this person **I am?** How does one

go from an intellectual level to experience the living reality of Self? It is the reality of beauty and serenity; this love of a loving kind, beingness of nature, is within, and one can sense it in the presence of utter silence. Self-inquiry into the core of **Who Am I** is a beautiful technique and shows results if practiced correctly. Wanderings in mind may bring about calmness and a feel-good awareness. Still, true contemplation of Self through inquiry within is a set expansive and fulfilling procedure, a method that involves timing.

Self-Inquiry will not be found by adding information. One will only see the untethered self by subtraction, by taking away all answers. Self-Inquiry diminishes the small self, the **I am** and is one of the most formidable forms of contemplation. It is not in the idle musings of the mind, which may feel good, but even calm and peaceful mind is not deep insight into the Nature of Reality. In Nondualism, the term for Self-Inquiry is Neti-Neti; not this, not this. It is inquiring into **who I am** from the perspective of questioning. Am I this, or this, or this? It is a progressive subtraction of concepts to arrive at a direct grokking when the ultimate reality of **who I am** is exposed. And if you think you've found an "answer," look again. More times than not, that exposure comes in a flash. Repeated self-inquiry meditation is good for getting that flash or "aha" moment, that epiphany, because it breaks through into the conscious mind. And that realization, however profound, does permeate the mind and comes to influence everyday activity. It reinforces and confirms that **who I am** is not this physical body. Glimpses like these, coupled with direct experience of Self through effortless meditation, help formulate an understanding of the nature of Self and recondition the mind to drop old belief systems, especially the belief that **I am the body.**

3. The last type of meditation is concentration applied; attention is focused with as much directed energy as possible to pierce through the veil of ignorance covering the true nature of reality. Concentration meditation aims to develop single-mindedness. The singularity of one's attention on an object, an image, one's breath, or a thought phrase can develop an ability to remain calm and grounded. Sometimes after a prolonged period of practicing directed concentration, the mind will automatically find a release, a letting go despite the practice, and will find a state of emptiness, resting within itself. An immediate transcending of objectivity to experience, not the rested grounded body but the ground state of mind. This kind of meditation typically either only sharpens the concentrative skills of the mind or produces a calm stillness of mind/body identification. It is challenging to transcend when one focuses or directs the mind outwardly or inwardly with any force.

4. Guided meditations are practical only so far as the meditation itself limits having a person experience the nature of the Self. The guided instructions are the limitation and can only point to something. Sure, anything is possible, and some people have had spontaneous awakening experiences through reading a passage in a book or listening to someone speak, but this is rare. The best and most effective results in guided meditations involve some healing modality expressed in the suggested words or instructions that bring about change through positive affirmation. Sometimes a dramatic change in a person on the psychophysiological level occurs from the produced healing. It is undoubtedly a good thing, and guided meditations have their place, especially with energy transmission-directed systems.

Maharishi Mahesh Yogi promoted group meditations right from the early days of the TM movement. Throughout his years as a spiritual leader, he would also send out groups of advanced meditators to hotspots in the world, areas exhibiting an overload of stress, political unrest, and evidence of a high crime rate. Various parameters of societal well-being were studied during and post periods of the regular group meditations. Meditation practiced regularly and in unison in these volatile civic areas showed a marked decrease in negative tendencies, and the results were statistically significant. With the scientific data collected and published, TM group meditations like these led to further investigation into this phenomenon. The power of people coming together in a group meditation setting amplifies exponentially the peace and silence experienced within that vicinity. Maharishi went on to say in his final years that it would be the packets of these types of meditator groups around the world that would have a high degree of positive influence and would change the course of world history.

> *Tat sannidhau vairatyagah* (Yoga-Sutra, 2.35)
> In the vicinity of coherence, Yoga, hostile tendencies are eliminated.

> As long as you believe that there is a progressive path and you have a way to go, then it will continue. But there is a direct path in transcending also; find out what is real. And be prepared to lose everything because you will lose everything of what you thought you were. —Jac O'Keefe

The various paths and the meditation outlined so far in the Nondual teachings and the journey to Self-realization are recorded in the historical records of Indian Philosophy, primarily in the Vedic texts dating long before Adi Shankara's period of disseminating the truth of Advaita. Yoga, or the union of life, is the realization of Self and is based on four distinct methodologies of gaining supreme knowledge:

Raja Yoga, the royal path yoga of meditation, was originally only given to Rajas, the royalty of society. It incorporates all the other paths to establish an approach representing the natural flow of creation: Mantra, Kundalini, Karma, Bhakti, and Hatha Yoga meditations. The fundamental principle was to become comfortable and investigate the depths of silence achieved through various spiritual practices. One appreciates and becomes the inner **"I"** sense quality as one transcends into silence. Raja Yoga is also known as Ashtanga Yoga; the eight limbs of Yoga describe the internal, external, and ethical dispositions of Yoga from Patanjali's Yoga Sutras. The most important of these is the eighth limb, Samadhi, or absorption in Oneness. The other limbs include Yama (abstinences), Niyama (observances), Asana (postures), Pranayama (breath control), Pratyahara (sense withdrawal), Dharana (concentration), and Dhyana (meditation).

Karma Yoga is the path of action and perception of doing and experiencing the journey, not the destination. A visceral seeing activity through the lens of right or wrong movement maintains a balanced perspective on choices made in line with one's Dharma and the unfolding evolutionary progress.

Bhakti Yoga is the path of devotion where the heart expands, feelings and emotional energies are supported by love and moved by love. One recognizes the Divine intervention in all things. Perceiving the Divine Presence in everything, one's heart expands in love and becomes one with that expansive energy.

Gyan Yoga is a path of the intellect, discernment, and discrimination of the known. The study of ancient scriptures espousing truth and its relevance to one's appreciation of evolutionary life cycles and the expansion of consciousness, *the Crest Jewel,* one pierces sharply through the veil of ignorance.

Yoga philosophy contains subtle variations within each methodology that promotes spiritual growth. A common theme is one's astrological chart or Jyotish, "the science of light." It is a means to mitigate adversity and subscribe to useful life indicators expressed through the alignment of the heavens. The configuration of the Planets exhibited in one's Natal Chart, or their expression at any given moment in time (Transits), reflects dominant subtle energies that are influencing the mind/body/organism. Knowing such information on time allows astrological remedial measures, or the very least enables one to move in the right direction to avert any not-so-favorable influence.

In compilation, Indian philosophy and the Vedic tradition of Yoga presented a means to gain Self-realization but was recognized as only a part of verifying knowledge as truth. During that period, an investigative procedure also emerged that integrated Yoga and the Six Systems of Vedic Philosophy to realize Truth on the objective level of reality. The postulate is that Ultimate Truth is found within existence as it appears. Superficial knowledge masks the Truth but maintains integrity with Truth in appearance. A command is valid only when seen and verified in the light of the Six Systems of Indian philosophy.

1. NYAYA – The science behind the reasoning. Correctness of the procedure to investigate objective knowledge. The justice in the rules of method in acquiring the Truth.

2. VAISHESHIKA – Criteria for the analysis to differentiate objective reality. Identify the object of inquiry beyond any doubt—perception and inference are based on reducible parameters of inherent qualities to distinguish objectivity.

3. SANKHYA – Enumerates the object of an immediate investigation into its component values. Primarily consciousness is layered from pure existence to the manifest material in an ordered sequential unfolding that distinguishes Truth as dualistic and Oneness simultaneously.

4. YOGA – Direct cognition of objective reality through refined perception as achieved through the union of Shiva and Shakti, silence and dynamism, subjective reality, and objective reality is seen as one Consciousness.

5. KARMA MIMANSA – Close consideration and study of objective knowledge. Modes of activity of the object and its components. A critical investigation into the ritual of action.

6. VEDANTA – Exposition of the object's reality in its phases as Absolute Truth. The discrete relationship between Brahman and Atman. The end of the Veda, the culmination of existence as Oneness.

One can easily see that knowledge of the reality of life some thousands of years ago was not taken lightly when the investigation into the truth of objective life was concerned. A highly skilled and self-aware society relied on living facts and understanding the reality of Oneness. The systems involved were of the highest caliber and, if studied, go beyond what is available in today's science. In his restoration of the Vedic tradition in gaining knowledge, Maharishi Mahesh Yogi called it Vedic Science, experientially verified understanding of ancient scriptures and texts.

Self Inquiry, Non-Duality's Flagship.

Self-Inquiry, part of the contemplative meditation platform, stands alone as a meditative technique. It shines in its own right. Self-Inquiry is just that, inquiring into the nature of Self. What is the Self? Can one get a handle on it, this short subject called consciousness? We all know it is there; we all have this sense of being, but where is it? What is it? Non-Duality and Self-Realization are synonymous, and Self-Inquiry is the search and exposition of Consciousness and Oneness.

Self-Inquiry is the hallmark of Nonduality teachings; it dates back to Adi Shankara and, more than likely, before that. Historically, we can only go back so far, but if the Veda are implied to be eternal and correct in the ancient wisdom and truth contained and expressed, then the adage of "nothing is new under the sun" holds fast. In the field of universal memory, the Smritis, or the Akashic field, then Self-Inquiry is a self-evident all-time reality. Think of it metaphysically and not on the level of personal meditation. What is the vastness of Source energy promoting by manifesting the potential of creation, none other than the inquiry into **itself**?

When I wrote earlier in the section about the ego/mind, it was brought out that the first identification is the, **I am**. It is quickly followed by the **I am the body** idea, and more quickly, the vision **I have to do something about it**. It is the primary veil of ignorance or identification and attachment that leads one down the path of pain and suffering. Self-Inquiry is established as a means, along with other modalities, to see beyond the veil and find peace, peace of mind.

> There is no peace of mind; there is either peace or
> mind.   —Ramana Maharishi

It all comes down to feeling and being the separate self, with a presumption of free will and a conceptual reality of **I am the doer** of the action. These are the ideas and belief structures set up at an early age in life. From this limited perspective, we associate whatever is present in our perceptual awareness and give it this false meaning.

Self Inquiry is tricky because the ego/mind is involved in the inquiry, and its primary pact or operating agreement is to maintain control. If it feels threatened with loss of control, it will find a myriad of ways to convince you of its sovereignty and solidity. The mind only recognizes the expansion and contraction movement, the Universal law of evolutionary force. With the expansion, the ego/mind will automatically, through thought, bring about doubt and confusion about what is occurring because expansion indicates truth reality, and this is counter to the mind's limited set of beliefs. With contraction, the false reality sense of self is dominant. The narrow mind relishes this objective surface value of the evolutionary cycle because it confirms its integrity as a controller. And as the presumed doer, it promotes the recycling of the never-ending loop of identification through claiming authorship.

In Self-Inquiry, one must learn to trust in the discernment of what feels expansive and what feels contracted. Limiting beliefs in **separation, doer ship,** and **the body** is the ego/mind's way of reinforcing the ignorance of the self as a constraint and insignificant. Contemplations and thoughts about the actual reality of life are expansive and self-affirming to guide and break the conditioning through limiting beliefs.

Self-Inquiry as a practice for revealing the true nature of Self is very helpful. The questions of **who am I**. "Who is experiencing this or that?" "Who cares" and "What then?" empower self-expansion. While effective in the inquiry process, these questions can sometimes be hijacked by the limited ego claiming to be spiritual and claiming any false affirmation that may arise to appease the investigation. The crafty side of the ego/mind should not be underestimated. But it is not at war with you, fighting for supremacy in limitations. It is just functioning as it has for millennia out of self-justifying conditioning to circumstance, a means to recognize and find purpose, and this strengthens the belief that the ego is a real, solid "thing." It is a misperception, a notion that doesn't exist in the way ego wants us to believe it exists.

Do not fight the ego; it will only strengthen its limitation. If it feels like a contraction, then the awareness should stop the inquiry and settle into that simple state of existence or being for a short period. Breathe slow complete breaths through the back of the heart and out the front at least four times depending on the contraction, and watch it dissipate. It will, in time, settle anyway. Then continue with the practice of Self-inquiry to root out the false ego.

Self-inquiry is an eyes-closed contemplation of Net-Neti, not this, not this, begins by acknowledging that "I am not the body or its parts." Then continues this process moving progressively inward. "I am not the mind and its thoughts or beliefs." Not ego and its authorship, and not the intellect and its piercing conclusions. Not the emotions and sensations that confirm any energy transfer. This is the general framework of inquiry, but guidance is necessary because words and timing play a role. Through this process, one settles into simple awareness, and the question of "who am I?" is laid bare as "I-ness." The result is the calmed Self-awareness of itself. When awareness settles down to itself in this manner, and recognition alone is established, then simply rest there, in that indescribable feeling of Self. Self is revealed as stillness, silence, and mystery. At first, it may be a brief flash followed by the thought, "what was that?" Remember that pure awareness of Self has no attributes. It's your true absolute nature. Also, while quickly lost, the flash experience of Self will expand with continued practice.

Self-inquiry from the angle of Neti-Neti, not this-not this, is a valid practice. But one must know who is doing the asking. Is it the ego/mind, or is it coming from a deeper, more universal place? In quiet meditation, this may be apparent, but it can also be practiced with eyes open and as a function in daily routine. Of course, if attention is required in critical or intense situations, Self-inquiry will mostly be mute. These eyes open Self-Inquiries should be practiced as a free-flowing attitude of simple awareness behind the scenes of perception of the phenomenal world. The philosophy or observation is that the objective world is a positive illusion of consciousness and is an appearance of life but not indicative of the deepest levels of reality.

Once one sees through the illusion of "me" as separate from outer reality, one enters a gateway to understand and realize that conscious awareness stands as the One witnessing all phenomena, including the mind-body organism. It is the actual reality of the Self. The Self, or pure awareness, is whole and complete. It simply observes. It does not care about analyzing the process or practicing self-inquiry; it observes what unfolds. However, Self-inquiry allows a glimpse and a feel for expanded awareness. Intimacy with truth arises along with this expansion. Joy, bliss, and energy emerge with this knowing of Self. This recognition is a living reality. The phenomenal world is as it truly is; one self-interacting dynamic. Oneness and everything expressed within Oneness is, as it should be, a happening in the flow of life. Self-Inquiry can lead to such an awakening or seeing. However, the work is not over. It is just the beginning of the journey.

> It's important to note, as well, that we do not become immune to misperception simply because we've had a glimpse of awakening; certain fixations and conditioning will linger even after we perceive from the place of oneness. The path after awakening then is a path of dissolving our remaining fixations—our hang-ups, you might say.   — Adyashanti

The work is not over means that all the parts within the Wholeness of Oneness have not been realized in their essential nature as pure consciousness within that motion of consciousness from Source eternal. The movement of expansion and contraction is the ever-evolving progress of existence to know itself in whatever capacity. You are that capacity and can realize the highest knowledge of Self as a human being. Of course, from the perspective of infinity, and all contained manifest reality, it seems unlikely that all specific parts of objectivity altogether in one smash instant could realize the ultimate Wholeness. It doesn't have to because its connection with Source is already whole and complete at its point value. The human being has the capacity and can awaken to this reality and live it knowing everything as Self—manifest consciousness in motion in one vast ocean of Wholeness.

The individual mind/body organism and its place in the evolutionary scale of life and its relationship to consciousness, the human being, has been gifted as a species. Through the Creator's grace, we can reach and realize the highest truth available in this reality we call life. Life as expressed by Source energy, Wholeness, God, Divinity, call it what you may. It is reported in ancient scriptures and through current awakening experiences that the journey is never finished. The unfolding of ever-increasing qualities of realization of

Oneness, the infinity beyond all words and conception, the vision of always more openings and awakenings are available.

Whatever we are striving for or have realized as a continuing expansion in awareness, the unfolding journey, as seen through Nonduality, is one of the Mind-Heart-Gut openings of conscious awareness. This mapping of consciousness has been described by Adyashanti, a well-known Zen/Nondual teacher from America. I find it very well laid out, and his expression coincides with the TM model of higher states of consciousness taught by Maharishi Mahesh Yogi.

They compare these three areas of mind, heart, and gut, as intelligence centers historically back to the Greeks, Egyptians, and Vedic India. These three locations correspond with chakra centers and encompass an area vertical to the spine and to the outer limits of the physiology at that point. The Crown chakra represents the mind, the Heart chakra, the heart center, and the Sacral chakra is the gut. At an outer area from these three chakra centers is a corresponding energy control point known as Mahamarmas in Indian philosophy. And they turn the energy wheels of the chakras to reflect the Marmas specific energy: Sthapati—Head, Hridaya—Heart, and Basti—Gut. There is a delicate yet profound connection between consciousness and physiology at these points.

Modern science also has a hand in this integrated phenomenon connecting the three with neuron count and mutual interoperability. Surprisingly enough, it has been known for some time now that the heart co-exists intimately with the brain in sympathetic neuron firing. The gut is currently being explored more thoroughly, and to date, the ENS or Enteric Nervous System, the Gut, rivals the brain in neuron count. Something is unique to this Mind-Heart-Gut-Consciousness connection, and when seen in comparison to the seven states of consciousness proposed by Maharishi, it makes sense.

Initially, it is the Mind level of consciousness recognition where one realizes without a doubt that the **I am** is just pure **I-ness** as consciousness; when the Crown Chakra has opened to the degree that Self-realization has dawned. Consciousness has woken up to itself and the recognition that Self is a container of awareness where the mind/body and the surrounding environment are an automatic display of activity going about in the same daily routines and expressions as before. It is freedom of sorts, but as one teacher put it, it's a kind of enlightened ignorance. In the sense that the value of an awakened reality of Self has been set free to know itself, however, the other aspect, the apparent material world of manifestation including the mind/body, which continues as it always has, is a mystery. Its destiny includes a profound purpose in the progression of evolutionary spiritual unfoldment; something within physical creation holds the key to a deeper understanding of reality.

The next awakening is from the opening of Heart consciousness. It comes online in an energetic display of the power of the Heart Chakra. The Heart energy is love-bliss, the Ananda aspect of Source's three-fold, Sat-Chit-Ananda qualities. Open and flowing with expanded consciousness, this love is the grand unifying principle in life. God is Love. Love is God. When fully realized and embodied in the psychophysiological functioning of the nervous system, the consciousness of Self sees from this perspective that the material manifest environment is also none other than Consciousness. One experiences the Self in everything. Clarity has been established in the certainty that everything is non-other than Consciousness, and it's one ocean in motion of wholeness or Oneness.

The final, but not so final, is the Gut awakening. We will detail this awakening later in the book's sections because it entails a lengthy explanation of consciousness's very intricate mechanics—from this awakening stage, ambiguity and paradox reign supreme. We could say that the Gut opening in Nonduality is the realization of Brahman in the Vedic knowledge perspective, the perception of the all-ness.

One must carefully consider this road to Nondual reality that everything counts even though nothing matters when seen through the illusion of life. The material and manifest illusions play a vital role in developing higher states of consciousness. How could it not? It's all consciousness, nothing but consciousness. Consciousness displays itself through Maya the illusion. Let us bring it right down to the individual mind/body organism, illusory but vital, nonetheless. As mentioned, this precious mind/body is the vehicle through which consciousness expresses itself to know itself. Suppose this vehicle is run down, full of stress, affected by Karmic impressions individually and collectively. What chance does it have to be the most delicate receiver/transmitter of pure consciousness? The work has yet to be done, even after initial Self-realization or awakening. And it is done by cleansing and clearing the stuck energies.

Here is where healing modalities come into play; psychological and physical, mental, or bodily; it's all related to energy healing on various levels of the mind/body. Later in this section, we will go into the different healing techniques, but now is a great time to explain the most used method in the Nondual teachings related to the conscious awareness field of mind/body, Shadow Work. This work directly addresses the Karmic imprints buried in the subconscious that affect our daily reality. Not all these Samskaras, latent impressions, have been released through an awakening, the first stages of Self-realization. One can live in the freedom and security of an abiding awareness of Self, but the mind/body through which this free awareness is channeled or operating could be unhealthy. The same old characteristics and traits continue, and it is because of the long-standing conditioning yet to be healed and released buried deep in the subconscious.

In some present-day iterations of Nonduality teachings, Shadow Work Healing has been incorporated as a leading stay practice. Coveted historical Advaita/Vedanta teachings, including prominent Gurus such as Ramana Maharishi, Nisargadatta Maharaj, and their disciples focused primarily on awakening, Self-realization first and foremost. A more modern integrated well-being approach to spirituality is prevalent where various healing modalities are offered, and Shadow Work is quite popular. Carl Jung first coined the term shadow. He noticed that the self-projected aspects of the psyche were playing around in the unconscious mind. The word shadow expresses those aspects of ourselves that have not yet been fully brought into the light of awareness.

These fundamental shadow aspects bring about dark and destructive behavior, limiting our natural evolutionary progression. The crux is that we remain completely unaware of what the cause is. We are taught what we know by conditioning from an early age. Some good, some very incongruent about who we are and what we are. Even more so, many of our feelings are deemed acceptable, which imprints deeply on the emotional body. We naturally suppress those feelings because it is our nature to desire acceptance. These feelings are banished into our subconscious because we want acceptance and love in our social domain. They become a part of our shadow side. Anytime you have had an emotional reaction to something that was seen as unfavorable, your conscious mind takes control and does not allow that which it does not want to experience to surface. It relegates that experience, that part of your psyche, into an energetic negative energy vibration locked within your subconscious, along with the multitude of other impressions in which some are positively polarized and are benign.

The distorted negative energy slowly wreaks havoc on your perception of reality by resurfacing the power like a mirror of life circumstances. Ego constantly living in the past or the future triggers these impressions to be seen as a movement forward. Still, we inevitably, through the limited awareness of ego/mind, the opposite occurs, and we again suppress the emotion or blame it on the other depending on the interpretation of the ascribed circumstance.

There are three stages of shadow Work as clinically expressed by Carl Jung. Over the years, there have been modifications, and what I am sharing represents the current thinking. It's practical and straightforward to understand. Applying it as part of Nondual teaching and a healing modality supports the growth of conscious awareness to expand beyond the limitations and constraints that the ego/mind places on reality.

Stage One. – Awareness –

Notice what your triggers are. When they arise, be completely present with what you feel and look straight at them. The stimulus and the feeling or sensation behind it will show itself partially or sometimes fully. Whatever the case, allow yourself to feel the partial or full arising thoroughly. Remember, the ego/mind is reluctant to project negative impressions because the resulting experience is guilt or shame. The function of the ego/mind is such that beliefs arise automatically through the triggers, but whether the arising is seen entirely depends on one's strength and clarity of conscious awareness—the greater the feeling, the greater the healing. Open yourself up completely, even if the pain associated with the sense is unbearable. Dive into it and express it in whatever way it comes up, even if it seems outlandish or embarrassing. Feel it as if it is outside the body as well, getting in touch with the full scope of that energy signature.

Stage Two. – Forgiveness –

Forgiveness is an act of reconciliation that dissolves the illusion of separation by recognizing that I am not separate from this pain and suffering, even though I may reject and run away from these negative feelings. Conversely, getting so caught up in self-gratifying activity leads to behavioral addiction. Through love and compassion, by welcoming the trauma fully and accepting it in whatever form it presents itself, you can easily share it as part of yourself and forgive it and yourself for not understanding the valid message behind the ego/mind shadow dynamics. It is the role of Samskara, the shadow, and Sadhana, the spiritual progress, to achieve positive movement naturally on the path to Self-realization. Know it as a good thing and forgive; the ego automatically wants to forget.

Stage Three. – Integration –

After every healing session, take some time to sit back and say thank you to the pain, to see that this once negative hidden aspect of yourself was there to serve you in seeing and letting go of the original trauma or negative impression. It was there all along to help you and not to hurt you. In this way, you can integrate its healed remnants and have closure, receiving that part of yourself you were not loving. Thank it for the invaluable lesson of self-healing. This forgiveness and thanking of trauma and its healing bring about a robust quality in the Heart called gratitude. It is key. When the heart fully expresses gratitude for the healing process, seeing how the apparent separation caused by the trauma has been dissolved, consciousness on whatever level recognizes itself as Oneness.

With energy self-healing, we must be patient because the complexity and depth of the trauma or negative conditioning are unknown. One or two healing sessions may seem complete, especially if the release was dramatic. Still, one may find that reflective parts of the Samskara, psychophysiological imprints, may resurface again in some form. We are all works in progress. Suppose we hold patience with a loving attitude towards the shadow side of our psyche and any corresponding triggered feelings. In that case, through genuine forgiveness, we can see through the delusional games of the ego/mind.

> There is no coming to consciousness without pain. People will do anything, no matter how absurd, in order to avoid facing their own Soul. One does not become enlightened by imagining figures of light but by making the darkness conscious.
>
> —C. G. Jung

The forgiveness stage is the turning point in Samskara/Sadhana dynamics in understanding false identities of ego/mind and its delusion in dealing with any experienced recurring life trauma. Forgiveness is the most challenging practice; it is the ultimate assault on the individual ego's integrity and the illusions it has built. The ego cannot forgive because it only sees separation. The ego would instinctively forget rather than forgive. And to remember forgiveness is not the act of superficial acknowledgment that something wrong has been done to you, and the response is that's okay.

It is on a higher level; true forgiveness does not ask you to accept what someone or some action did. It asks you to see that nothing can ever be done to you, in your freedom of knowing that you are immutable pure Awareness at the depths of your being, and nothing can touch, stain, or harm this. You can give space to others acting out of their constraints and limitations. You understand now, with love, that whatever we go through is our process of growth. Forgiveness also asks you to stop seeing yourself as independent or separate and stop believing the ego's lie that you are a victim.

From a Nondual perspective in the reality of Oneness, there arises fundamental recognition of the parts. Primarily knowing that life's unfolding display is transitory. All activity, including any wrongdoing, is valid. More so, action is not happening to the Self but is just an expression of your consciousness in motion. Forgiveness on that level is the gratitude that I am alive, living this incredible journey called life. Forgiveness is an easy and powerful tool on that level of recognition. This highest recognition is that no one can ever attack me. They can only attack the illusion that they think I am. Maharishi used to distinguish levels of identification as either a line drawn in rock or one in the sand, better yet one outlined in the air.

Forgiveness is the ultimate act of self-love. You forgive the other and yourself, which means any hidden trauma can be reconciled in any shape or form because you see through the delusion. You also know that any apparent trauma is essentially none other than yourself in a unique format. Love and forgiveness are towards yourself, so in actuality, love and forgiveness are an act of receiving.

> The act of forgiveness vibrates in the high energy of spiritual consciousness.
> —Paramahansa Yogananda

Self-healing energy transformation work is a tremendous and essential supplement in aiding the progress of Self-realization. The Oneness of Nondual reality inherently suggests that true wholeness incorporates all the parts in that Oneness perspective. Everything is valid by its sheer expression, and there is no shortage of self-serving people out there who may mean well, but the bottom line is always for themselves. Common sense and informed decision-making, thorough research about all the healing claims, and promised states of well-being out there are prudent. Naivety and innocence are no excuse.

Holistic approaches to energy healing which are based ultimately on service to others even though you are working on yourself, represent the true nature of Oneness. We are all the same consciousness; what I do for myself in raising my energy vibration to the highest level possible, I am doing for the other, which is none other than myself. It's all Oneness; it's all valid. Oneness does not distinguish between good and evil. However, the choice made is the choice given and produces the results of either service to a small sense of self or service to others.

There are many strata to creation, as material science and metaphysical science reveal the makeup of the psychophysical expression of the human being. Healing can be derived through techniques that target any imbalance at any of those accepted levels. Many energy healing modalities are available, either as self-help or guided by a qualified, reputable healer. Talented and capable healers range from modern scientific psychoanalytical doctors and psychologists to metaphysical and even esoteric healing practitioners.

If one wants work done in this area, all one must do is Google, place it in context, and investigate the healing modality thoroughly to know it is genuine.

The importance from a Nonduality standpoint is that the first initial awakening to Self, where one is recognized as **I am not the body** separate from the other, is fundamental in the evolutionary progress forward. This initial Nondual recognition of Self has served humanity through the ages, to bust through the ignorance of the ego/mind. Everything seems relatively automatic after the first awakening; therefore, choices express what arises from that perspective. The choice made was inevitable. At that point, any energy self-healing work on the personal mind/body automatically appears. Before the awakening, there would be more identification with "this wounded self" that needs healing. This narrow view may lead to unnecessary suffering, but healing modalities before and after any awakening are choices made.

Healing modalities, whether self mode or guided, and it doesn't matter whether you got it from a teacher, a book, or you are lying on a couch being analyzed; it is personal work. Sitting in a lotus position, transcending perception, stretching in a Yoga posture, suspended in a water tank, receiving energy transmission, or sitting in the rays of your Master's darshan, all these modalities are your work and some form of Sadhana. You must see evidence of growth and healing within yourself. An immediate visceral experience or recovery may appear sometime after an integration period. It's all out there, many varied ways to heal the "inner child."

During this present time in the world around us, the evolutionary process has brought a significant number of the population an awareness to break free into something more relevant and in tune with higher spiritual energy. Even so, most have that subtle inner impetus to be a better version, complete and fully healed. Don't let the ego snatch that away in the guise of constant spiritual seeking and searching for the subsequent best healing. Find what works for you and become devoted to yourself and humanity's spiritual journey.

Nonduality teachings offer a straightforward realization of reality, simply recognizing that **I am not the body** is a starting point. Simple yes, but only recognizable to the degree it is. Behind the hardened conditioned belief that you are an independent body within a separate world is the collective consensus reality and your specific Samskaras. Nondual teachings provide an approach to living the highest. It does take commitment and some lifestyle changes, but it can be incorporated as an easy routine without the burden of becoming overly one-pointed and acting like an ascetic. One can carry on the path of Sadhana recognition every moment if you like because it is happening anyway. Giving attention to the principle of Sadhana expands the conscious awareness to be more present. Reconditioning the narrow-centered ego/mind is as natural as the initial conditioning was from birth.

> The undoing of domination by the mind can be accomplished by one single step, "humility," which is reinforced by simply recognizing that the mind is not sovereign, omniscient, or even capable of telling the truth from falsehood. —David Hawkins

There is a depth of guidance in humility if one returns to the realm of consciousness, where you understand and know that you are only a tiny part of the Divine play. Within the vulnerability of humility, one hears the voice of Atman, the Soul, and its connection with Totality. Humility shines on this level of integrated conscious awareness as the dominant feature of existence and moving forward towards Self-realization that will allow you to know your actual value, worth, and understanding of why you are here.

VI. ENLIGHTENMENT—THE MAP OF CONSCIOUSNESS

Enlightenment from a conceptualized viewpoint has been batted around for centuries, if not longer. Many individual cultural representations have tried to shine a light on this concept. Whatever has been said from authentic experience can never really get across the defining limitations of speech. Language, the driving force in the evolution of humanity, can only describe enlightenment to the degree words can offer to the experience, and there lies the paradox of reality. The so-called enlightened person is just a limited expression of the realized Self. Maya, illusion, while being an essential dynamic within the presentation of enlightenment, is not and cannot become enlightened. It can at one point vibrate in the frequency of the highest Truth but will remain as an illusion. The limitations of language are restricted to the physical domain and can only shine forth a possible best description of Absolute reality but cannot know the ultimate truth. Oneness, Nondual ultimate reality stands alone; nothing else can be said about it; the moment one tries, it is duality.

Enlightenment is a perfect word to point toward shining light on something which is not a thing but hidden in all things. From a relative perspective, the light of consciousness is expressed in stages. They are signposts that one's expansion experience moves towards the highest goal available in quest for ultimate reality. Inevitably enough, experiences of higher or greater stages of consciousness with their varied qualities and personal evaluations have all gone into the mix in structuring a sort of hierarchy in the advancement toward the totality of consciousness. It has left many original intentions as to which stage is what and where they fit into other experiences of the highest realization. All this is placed into a historical context of revelations about enlightenment from scripture. Only one thing is sure and can be agreed upon, that ultimate reality is unknowable. There is a spiritual caveat "to know it; you have to be it." It's difficult to say for sure, but I believe very few human beings in recorded history have reached an ultimate divine level of enlightenment that resonates with Totality.

It is quite interesting because today, there is a quickening happening in the world despite all the chaos. More and more individuals are waking up to an abiding awareness of Self-realization. In addition, from the groups I have encountered and been involved with, more people also have very high levels of awakening. Even though my friends and I come from a spiritual background from the late 60s, if it was not for this high energy hastening and all the synchronicity appearing in our lives currently, the thought of writing a book may not have materialized. A close friend of mine said, "we get the call, and surprising things arise."

All spiritual seekers express what enlightenment may mean to them based on their ongoing experiences, and whatever lineage or teaching predominates their outlook. All the self-realized indicate what that seeing or unfolding is from their level of consciousness.

The more realized you become, the more you are a mystery. As the layers of misperception fall away in the expansion of consciousness, you find that the infinite, unbounded consciousness you are in the mystery unfolding. The more one sees through the illusion, the more the mystery is revealed. The secret is you know you are the mystery, but now you are living that mystery. The realization of "I am that," but what is that? The "what" is buried deep in that mystery of Self. The more unraveling of the "what" you are, the more the value of liberation. It is all about Moksha, ultimate liberation where one relinquishes *Artha,* the means of life, the Kama, the passion of desire, and then the depths of righteousness that reign supreme begin to reveal a secret. The secret of who you truly are unfolds in layers or qualities of freedom and expansion beyond imagination along the journey. The joy of the puzzle has come a long way from the suffering of certainty.

> Give up identification with this mass of flesh as well as with what thinks it a mass. Both are intellectual imagination. Recognize your true self as undifferentiated awareness, unaffected by time, past, present, or future, and enter Peace.
> —Adi Shankara

Historically, the map of consciousness unfolding to itself through the expansion in conscious awareness of the individual has, in general, been the same. The journey and signposts are similar because the evolutionary forces guide or unfold consciousness through the totality of the energy frequency and vibration that make up the entity we call a human being. Any differences or uniqueness of individual psychophysiology only plays a minor role. The journey is the same; however, the footsteps along the path will differ. It's good to understand these signposts or stages of expanding consciousness. As stated, the Nondual map of consciousness unfolding into a greater understanding of self and an appreciation of actual reality comes in three stages of development. Although more elaborate in presenting a map of consciousness expansion, Vedic philosophy is similar to these three stages.

1. *Mind Awakening,* or Self-realization, where the true nature of Self is recognized as unbounded, infinite conscious awareness, and the realization of endless intimacy with Self has always been the case but forgotten. It is most natural; a definite shift has occurred, while everything seems to be the same, a recognition or realization that **I am not the**

body, I am not the doer becomes apparent. A fullness of awareness with consciousness dawns as Self. It is an unbounded, untouched awareness of Self. However, the perception of the environment remains the same. At the same time, there seems to be a disconnect between Self-awareness as the Observer and the Observed activity of the personal body and the movements of the seen environment. This perspective accents the dream reality of the material world. It seems like nobody is home; the drama of life unfolds spontaneously. This stage can also fluctuate because it is so new, and this awakening from the opening of the crown chakra does not mean other chakras are fully open and functioning in optimal balance. Reflections within the consciousness of Self may vary on an energetic level.

In Vedic Science, Maharishi called this description of Self-realization Cosmic Consciousness, the first stage in developing consciousness's highest realization and liberation. The true Self is recognized as unbounded, infinite, and Cosmic.

2. *Heart Awakening*, the Self-realization of the Unity of all things, is when one understands the depths of consciousness through natural intimacy and knowing consciousness as the Self. A constant meditation occurs after the initial self-realization, revealing the finer aspects of consciousness. This inward movement expands toward the **I-ness** that has dropped the **I am** but still resonates deep within consciousness. It's not a personal sense of **I** by any means; it transcends more as an absolute quality. Through this phantom presence of **I** that cannot be captured, consciousness is in the process of exploring itself. This movement in the exploration of the Self, consciousness naturally refines and adjusts the frequency vibrations of the mind/body organism:

the nervous system, chakras, and the subtle body energies sheaths.

With the combination of consciousness-expanding and the body coming online at a higher frequency vibration, especially the Heart Chakra, something exquisite happens. The individual's conscious awareness expressed as Cosmic Consciousness, or the infinite Observer recognizes that the environment, including the personal body, is also none other than the Self, a recognition of consciousness alone is. It is one consciousness, One-Self of everything, **I am of consciousness, and you are also consciousness.** It is the unity level of consciousness, the actual natural state of consciousness of the human being. It is where and when the journey begins.

In Vedic Knowledge and Science, Maharishi referred to this state as Unity Consciousness. There is also an intermediary stage before Unity that Maharishi called God Consciousness. It is where the unifying energies of the Heart are bringing together the Subject and Object as One. As this process develops, a rapport with the celestial energy level of reality may be seen or sensed in some value. A refined perspective reality or perception of angelic energies or beings may be appreciated during the unfolding of Unity Consciousness. There may also be an unexpected sense of devotion, or a feeling of sanctity, since the Heart's desire to unify differences moves consciousness to look deeper into the reality of Self, in ever greater expressions of humility and surrender to the Self.

3. *Gut Awakening* is the Self-realization of the holiness of life. The circle has been completed so far that the totality of consciousness is experienced in its fullness. The Infinite, unbounded consciousness has been established in awareness that everything is Self. Within the constant expansion of Self is seen a stirring from that mystery of **I-ness** on all levels. With a high clarity of consciousness, a refined perception reveals the **indweller** of existence, and it is seen as Totality.

What is that stirring of **I** that draws or expands consciousness to reveal ultimate truth? The point value of absolute infinity, the potential inherent in Source in the quality-less intention of emergence as the **I absent to itself**. This statement will only begin to make sense if one has a glimpse of the Self-realized state. It is sometimes reported as an unnerving experience when this ultimate stage of consciousness dawns. One passes through the gateless gate, the void of existence, the point value between Absolute and Relative, unmanifest and manifest, referred to in Indian philosophy as **"lamp at the door, inside light-outside light,"** and it is an end of your worldly experience. Therein rests the **I,** the gateway into the unknown dimension of nothingness. It's a divine beckoning from consciousness to look deeper into Self, this mysterious **I.** When one has this shift in consciousness from what in contemporary Nonduality is referred to as the Gut perspective, the realized Self loses everything. Being established in Unity Consciousness perspective, it loses the reality of Unity, the beingness of consciousness; it drops the **Is-ness** and the relative illusion of existence; everything vanishes in a vacuum, a void, only to return to a perspective reality of Brahman, the supreme absolute Totality.

First, there is a mountain; then there is no mountain, then the mountain returns.

—Buddhist Koan

Navo-Navo bhavati jayamanah   Rig Veda 10.85.19

In the process of transformation, or evolution, it is the Totality that is reborn again and again.

Sarvam Khalu Idam Brahm   Chhandogya Upanishad, 3.14.1

All this is Totality

Aham Brahmasmi Brihad-Aranyak Upanishad 1.4.10

I am totality

From that void of unknown nothingness, Oneness returns. Everything seems to be the same. The manifest reality remains, conscious awareness and the expanse of consciousness as everything is present, but everything, including the **I-ness** and existence, is appreciated as nothingness in appearance. It is the stage of consciousness that in Vedic Knowledge, and Maharishi Mahesh Yogi's teachings is termed Brahman Consciousness. As described through historical texts, Brahman is the highest principle or universal reality that comprises existence. Atman is the individuated Brahman that the human soul associates with the unbounded Self. So, the Atman realizes the totality of Oneness in the Gut awakening of Brahman Consciousness. It is coined the 'Gut' awakening because the Gut is where a connection to the intuitive resonance energy of the body is located. Remembering the Mind requires a body, and Spirit needs a Mind to know itself. Go with your gut, is a common saying. The Gut also represents the "middle earth" in mythology, the substantial essence of Mother Gaia in form. Mother Earth, where we human beings as a collective have been endowed and made this planet our home to evolve and grow spiritually. The collective Universal Dharma of our species.

This Gut area also is the home of the Navel or Sacral Chakra representing emotions and vitality; just below that is the Root Chakra, where survival instinct is dominant. Here is the crux of existence for the human being, a profound and concentrated tight-knit block of energy carried through lifetimes of the fear of death. Fear of losing presence and becoming nothing is ironic—that is just what occurs. It is the dropping away of everything and returning as the fullness of everything in the appearance of nothingness.

This "fear" is the last hurdle locked primarily in the lower two Chakras. It is the springboard in the evolution of consciousness for the human individual to realize something more significant, and that is Oneness shining as Oneness, Nonduality, the Ultimate reality. These are the teachings of Adi Shankara, Advaita /Vedanta, and Maharishi Mahesh Yogi's Vedic Science, where ancient meets modern understanding.

> Questions arise as to the Source of the capacity even to realize Existence or Beingness and whether such qualities are innate or are superimpositions by silent paradigm presumptions. One asks, "By what quality does the abstract even become discernable, and is not knowingness Itself merely a higher level of abstraction?" Again, although these queries may seem academic to the intellect, experientially, they are a priority and profoundly transformative as the light of the levels of Consciousness. At the highest levels, they represent the last cloud that hides the radiance of the Sun of Divinity. —David Hawkins

From the standpoint of the highest realization of Self, there is only one comprehensive meaning for Enlightenment. It says it all, even with all its ambiguity along the journey. It can be pronounced as the supreme existence, the absolute ultimate reality. What other conceptual meaning could you replace it with, other than Source? What else could it be? Genesis, the Fountainhead, Godhead, Divine Mother/Father. To be one with that, an intimate realization of that is the liberation of Atman— the individuated Soul shines in the light of Brahman. Within this field of Brahman, the unbounded, infinite, and vastness of nothingness is the seat of pure potentiality where the indweller is seen. Where potential existence as intent resides. Existence is none other than Source, and you are existence; you are Source. One must also keep in mind that these descriptions are not

Absolute values. We are speaking about the unmanifest, a field of nothingness; there are no values, no attributes.

Dure-drisham grihapatim atharyum Rig Veda, 7.1.1
Far in the distance is seen the owner of the house, reverberating.

When you stabilize in that beingness, it will give you all the knowledge and all the secrets to you, and when the secrets are delivered to you, you transcend the beingness, and you, the Absolute, will know that you are also not the consciousness.

Nisargadatta Maharaj

At Source, within Source, is the original inception, the indweller knowing itself, the pure field of consciousness, nothingness, the intent of becoming conscious as consciousness, the sense of being becoming. At that point of inception, which the Vedas call Para Pragya, *Para*: beyond, absolute; and *Pragya*: state of wisdom, which is higher than knowledge, intelligence, and understanding. This unimaginable Source, through the power of potentiality of Divinity, "the indweller" moves without moving, curving back on itself to know itself.

Source knowing itself or becoming pure consciousness is the initial act of creating. At this most refined and sublime level, existence vibrates at the highest frequency of light. This Para Pragya of the Veda is called the lamp at the door, "inside light-outside light." Source has curved back on itself to know itself, conscious of itself, a vast ocean of consciousness in motion. Consciousness means awareness of the pure potentiality inherent in Self. The vastness of infinite energy, silence, and liveliness contained within.

Source or the Ultimate Reality from a purely spiritual perspective, through the process of self-referral, the mystery of knowing itself as consciousness potential, is compelled by the emergence of energy inherent in consciousness to explore the full range of the infinite potential within itself. This movement of exploration to know itself fully shows itself as creative intelligence, the self-interacting dynamics, the power of manifestation at this subtlest level of source energy.

> I am the Para Prakriti (beyond phenomenal form, absolute form); at times, I appear with Gunas (qualities), and at other times I remain without Gunas. I am always of the causal nature; never am I of the nature of the effect. When I am causal, I am with the Gunas: when I am before the highest Purusha (pure abstract consciousness), I am without any Gunas on account of my remaining in the state of Samya Vastha (equilibrium).
>
> —Lucia Hoff

Source energy or pure consciousness is inherently self-referral, exploring its potential. Consciousness becoming Conscious, but there is that non-dimensional value of Source, that mysterious endpoint to all query, that elusive nothingness where one postulates origin—the holiness of Brahman, the Oneness beyond and behind manifestation.

Scientific investigation has not come close to verifiable proof beyond a mathematical description that falls short of any unifying principle. At the Planck epoch scale, just seconds before the "Big Bang," a state of singularity where space/time does not exist has been formulated. Scientific instrumentation currently available is not refined or precise enough to provide valuation at or beyond the Planck scale. Theoretically, a unified field is possible. The Large Hadron Collider (LHC) in Switzerland/France has established the "God particle," the missing theoretical Higgs boson, to complement the collapse of the wave function and add mass to elementary particles. Outstanding, adding mass to vibration, the process of manifestation, creation itself. Science is coming close, and theoretically speaking, the current thinking is exciting in defining a particular field that gives rise to the material realm.

Those who experience the Oneness of Life have attempted to express their insights in scriptures or poetry, ultimately admitting to language's limits. And without some personal glimpse of higher states of consciousness, it is difficult for someone reading those descriptions to understand.

Vedic Knowledge and the enormous volumes of text literature from scholars, along with possible remnants of that period in history where the rishis or seers of knowledge passed down the full expression of life to disciples, represented a lived reality. This daily quality of living was the actual value of Nondual reality and has been handed down through the generations to modern-day India and now to the world. Some parts of the written knowledge were not from the enlightened scholars of the time but from ordinary people, either monastic or otherwise, who lived the reality of higher states of consciousness and passed it verbally or in writing from their enclave. A rich history of truth has come from this Vedic Heritage. The Vedic understanding of Ultimate Reality came in two forms, spiritual and scientific, both experiential. Ancient India has been the home of esoteric knowledge and spiritual endeavors that permeate all strata of life, from kings to peasants.

Scientific investigation was being conducted, but as direct cognition of the dynamics of consciousness, mechanics of nature—the laws of nature which guide and propel life from the beginning. Arguably, what we call scientific instrumentation and postulated theories in advance were absent because the society at large was living at a much higher level of conscious awareness. It was an investigation from the subtle levels of creation, Source itself, through refined states of consciousness. Proof of verification through mathematics and modeled repeatable experimentation was not required. Direct cognition by the 'Rishi' or Seer from a state of consciousness that reflected the truth from that level was espoused, written, and shared.

Others verified this cognitive truth; by in large, society was a mirror of that lived reality. The investigation was self-evident. For many illustrious centuries, humankind lived in the freedom of Oneness, conscious of a higher reality

Of course, the modern worldview is skeptical where science and materialist perspectives are kings. Even though the scientific investigation has deeply penetrated reality, remarkedly so, it remains verified on a superficial level. However, if you are spiritually inclined and know something about the present-day theories of Quantum Physics, rest assured that things are headed in the right direction. From the scientific investigation and Quantum theories proposed into the nature and reality of what we call life over the past century, it is clear to see a very close and running parallel with the ancient spiritual views of truth. Primarily as one goes deeper into the physical dimension, the more unified the principles and laws of nature become, and the role of consciousness becomes more evident. The times they are quickening. We are entering a new age of science, and the study of consciousness is being recognized as primary to life and living.

Vedic Science, restored in its purity by Maharishi Mahesh Yogi, presents a beautiful expression of the dynamics of consciousness and the mechanics of nature, these natural laws that reside at the most refined levels of creation. These expressions of the Ultimate Reality of life or Oneness do justice to anyone awakening to those expressions of natural law because they are within us. They are us. We are the creators of reality in the final analysis. The Vedic Science understanding of creation as seen and revived by Maharishi translates in verifying that at that Planck scale where there is a unification of space/time, from that unified field, the laws of nature and its mechanics live in potentiality awaiting expression. They are all there, humming on that sublime level, intent on realizing their full potential. If you have ever wondered about the eternal sound of the universe as Aum, or commonly referred to as Om, that is the humming.

These laws of nature find expression in what Vedic Science refers to as the Veda, the blueprint of creation. From that level of Source potential, expressions of "sound-memory-origin" arise in genesis; Shruti, Smriti, Purananam, respectively. In classical spiritual terms, this is also the level of Sat-Chit-Ananda, purity-intelligence-bliss. Here sounds the Veda reverberating purity. The memory of the laws of nature in the potential that structure the entire creation, the "Big Bang."

Maharishi called these laws of nature the impulses of creative intelligence. Maharishi restored and described the Vedic literature in its purity and gave a more scientific connotation in expressing Vedic knowledge because he understood that science is now the backbone of human endeavor. It is the language of the time, and science must be respected. Maharishi's insight and contribution to humanity offered a direct, verifiable relationship between consciousness and physicality. It's quite simple; an intrinsic Absolute Source, pure consciousness, through post-creation synthesis, remains within us at a point value we call Self. We are all privy to it; we are it. The expansion of consciousness or the awakening to enlightenment realizes that level of being, the essence of who we are.

Anandaddhyeva khalwimani bhutani jayante anadena
Jatani jivanti anandam prayanty abhisamvishanti
Taittiriya Upanishad 3. 6. 1

Out of bliss, these beings are born, in bliss, they are sustained, and they go and merge again to bliss.

Within the realm of infinite potentiality springs creative intelligence, as described by Maharishi; these laws of nature manifest its source potential as the Universe, the unity inherent in the diversity of creation as Source. One important distinction that Maharishi brought out in his restoration in the purity of the Veda is that it is not only the reverberations of the sounds, Shruti, that structure manifestation, but the gaps between the sounds; Vedic knowledge call these gaps Brahmana. It is essentially Source energy at rest, Apaurusheya, the uncreated, which provides the truth that Source energy or pure consciousness is not only the substratum but pervades and permeates all of creation, even on the surface values of life.

It makes us realize that Source is pervading all material strata within the multi-various manifest expressions of creation. Within that energy configuration of the initial inception of the Self-referral or Self-interacting dynamics of consciousness, Maharishi calls it the Constitution of the Universal Laws of Creation. Source energy, the unified field, is home to these laws. Source energy explores the full range of potential within itself by manifesting its potential and realizing itself in that expressed potential as the joy of creating. This joy or Ananda bliss comes through creative intelligence inherent in the laws of nature. The laws of nature, or the mechanics, are governed from the "Devata" or celestial dimension of creation. Purity, Intelligence, Bliss abounds on this level. Sat-Chit-Ananda from Indian scriptures. In mythology, from this level of supreme energy, God's creation emerges, is sustained, and eventually will dissolve and return. The triumvirate of Brahma, Vishnu, and Shiva.

All expressions in creation are consciousness; consciousness is all there is. Consciousness becoming self-aware, or consciously functioning through us, only occurs in sentient beings. Not all expressions in creation are conscious enough for source energy to realize or know itself completely. That is why being a human being who can reflect the highest truth of Source or Oneness is so precious. It should not be wasted. All spiritual luminaries have endeavored to teach and revitalize awakening to this end. It is all dependent on the space/time continuum we were born in, the Age, the Epoch, in the evolutionary cycles of Consciousness if we can hear the calling. We have no control over it. As stated, the script has been written. Choices are made, there is a feeling of free will, but essentially it is the will of God, the self-interacting dynamics of the Constitution of the Universe. It is understood that we as human beings have the potential to rise to the status of Oneness, to know the Self completely. Shining as that highest reality, then why not capture that direction in whatever way feels the most comfortable.

> Life will give you whatever experience is most helpful for the evolution of your consciousness. How do you know this is the experience you need? Because this is the experience you are having at the moment. —Eckhart Tolle

Adi Shankara and his Nondual teachings were a part of this Vedic Heritage and knowledge. His teachings were an expression of his time when some values of Vedic knowledge were lost. The high energy vibrations of past societal awareness had subsided. The language to awaken people was more relevant in the personal experience of a limited ego/mind function that prevailed. The limitations in consciousness expressed during Shankara's time are similar to what is now occurring on the spiritual side of human evolution, mass ignorance coupled with the dawn of awakening. Most people are yearning for answers to existence and the why and what for, a meaning to life. People rarely introspect into these more essential questions, lost in their mundane world and driven by ego/mind.

The question of the reality of a state of Enlightenment for the human being and what it describes conceptually is again quite simple if one looks at the human condition progressively. "Happiness is not found through changing our external world, but through changing our internal landscape"—Shauna Shapiro. This beautiful saying is the turning point in awareness, and it comes at various stages in one's life, where understanding does turn back on itself ever so slightly to recognize that Self is calling to find the truth. Everything we have been searching for in the outer world is discovered within ourselves. From there on, the lived expression of that seeing is up for grabs.

But this is the starting point of what you may call a step towards the fullness of Enlightenment.

Whatever the journey, even if it is falling back again and rolling along with the norm or status quo, it does not matter. We are all headed in the same direction. Evolution's inherent power and grace always find balance and progress forward to uncover the Truth of existence. Be it a scientific or spiritual path, intellectual giants and seers of reality have proclaimed the divinity in all things from time immemorial. Knowingly, or unknowingly everything is spiritual. We are all in search of that one thing, something, whatever it may be, to find complete fulfillment in life. It does matter what path you take and how you take it. The opportunities are endless but choosing the most influential and practical spiritual journey is difficult for most, especially if one has ties to a strong family or cultural upbringing. As stated, everything is valid, regardless of whatever you do, and it is humbling and perfect for reminding oneself that you are already enlightened; you just forgot. And it's not the person who gets enlightened or awakened; it's the conscious awareness that wakes up to itself and to the illusion that there ever was an individual me.

One must ultimately drop everything. I mean everything; the whole wound-up conceptual in a nutshell idea and belief in a separate self, as it may be presented right now. Even from a relative standpoint, "No man/woman is an island unto him/herself,"—John Donne. Start by realizing the interwoven fabric of life, and it doesn't have to be on a high spiritual level. The internet, the world at your fingertips, the emergence of Web 3.0, and the immense globalization are but reflections of the growth seen in the unity of collective consciousness. And yes, it's also calling to take a deep look at yourself. Find the true reality of who you are. And don't worry, you won't lose your status or lovable characteristics; it will all come back online brighter and better. It's possible for some with a developed heart to feel that "sense of being" and feel into the devotion of that mystery within, then surrender to this mundane reality. An awakening can occur spontaneously, it's rare, but it happens. The majority of people involved in their busy lives who incorporate a spiritual practice will do so in stages, and that is perfectly fine.

I believe this book points out concisely that Non-Duality, Oneness is present all the time. It's just a matter of seeing that a Human is firstly a machine, as abrasive as that might seem, and the sense of the small self within and its projected illusory expressions is the gateway to the Self-realization of Source.

VII. DIVINITY,
SOURCE—COURSE—GOAL

"Knowledge is structured in Consciousness. Knowledge is different in different states of Consciousness," is something Maharishi Mahesh Yogi often said. Tied in with that, Maharishi also liked to say, "The world is as you are." The quality and characteristics of the knowledge of ultimate reality expressed and appreciated through your awareness or state of consciousness are the levels of clarity one reflects from pure Source into your truth. The source is the Source, and the Ultimate reality shines eternal, unperturbed. As a mind/body organism, you are but a reflector of that source, based directly on your nervous system's purity and style of functioning. Here, the nervous system means the total capacity expression from the subtlest layer to the gross structure aspect of the firing order of synapse-neuron vitality. Within the chakras, the most refined layers of energy frequency vibration, and how lively are the laws of nature on those levels operating and beyond. This mind/body is the hard-wired receiver/transmitter value in human consciousness, and your mind/body organism is a unique flower in God's Garden.

The relative expression of the complex inexplainable workings of Karma/Dharma, particularly your uniqueness, forms your world. Karma is the expressed activity displayed in the normal progression of the individual's life journey. Dharma is a Cosmic set of laws arising from memory for that individual. One could say that it is also Karmic impulses structured in a created order that is best suited in offering situations and circumstances in one's life to reflect the most transparent and best way forward. All the levels in adherence to and for a rapid evolutionary expansion of consciousness. In that remembering of Source expressing as your individuality, your clarity of consciousness is still intimately related and subject to the energy frequency vibration of Source in that memory, the wholeness or oneness of all that is. This memory value, expressed as individual Karma/Dharma, is a thread in consciousness connected to the "I-ness" of the individual that transcends to the Brahman quality of nothingness.

In **I-ness** rests memory in a solemn form of recognition, a getting ready for the rite of passage. It awaits volitional fruition to emerge as an individual mind/body organism. Of course, the manifestation steps are intricate. Vedic literature attributes thousands of pages to this subject, but it is safe to say the possibility from a "no-thing" to something is instantaneous. All opportunities are present in a state of potential and a form of manifest reality; paradoxically, nothing has ever happened in that vacuum of Brahman. It's that spinning coin again, don't try to figure it out. You can't. Every stage of reality has its own set of perspectives, "to be it is to know it."

> The infinite I is that subjective reality that underlies the individual I and allows for the experience of I-ness as one's existence. It is the absolute I that enables the statement, I am. Consciousness, or the capacity for awareness, is formless and is the backdrop from which form can be identified. That knowingness that arises from within is innate, accessible, and experiential. Such knowingness is beyond definition or description as the primary, confirmable, universal substrate of power and energy, out of which arises the possibility as well as actualization.   —David Hawkins

The journey never ends in the evolution of consciousness; this is a statement expressed by many, if not all, spiritual masters and teachers. The various maps of consciousness attest to the stages of development and qualify these levels by adding that there is always more clarity within each stage. So why would that not be the case when referring to Ultimate Reality? That would be equivalent to placing a definitive boundary on something infinite and containing all possibilities.

> Brahman is real. The world is not real. The world
> is Brahman.   —Shankara

And just when one was trying to wrap their head around nothingness, the supreme Brahman, the Ultimate Oneness of Nonduality, in comes something we have heard all too often, Divinity. Divinitatis, the derivative noun from Latin, meaning Godhead. English etymology places Divinity as a position of God. Therefore, when uttered, we all assume that Divinity has something to do with the heavenly realm, God the creator with divine holistic powers. Omnipresence, Omniscience, and Omnipotence. Within the Nonduality circle, as is with other spiritual teachings and ancient lineages, the word Divinity is used often, sometimes without knowing what the background or experiential reference is or was. In the context of this section, titled Divinity, the term announces the pinnacle of spiritual attainment if there is such a thing because it is the next stage within Brahman, aptly called ParaBrahman. One could use these terms interchangeably, but to pay homage to the Vedic Tradition, Shankara, and modern-day teachings in Nonduality, let's keep Divinity as another layer of the holiness of Self-realization.

The practice of Nondual teachings requires earnestness, devotion, and commitment of attention to that elusive sense of being, the **I-ness** within. This attention will enliven dormant energies silently waiting in rest. Instead of focusing on the constant chattering of the ego/mind, the journey to Self-realization can actualize as an abiding truth in reality. As one goes through the developmental stages of consciousness expansion and integration, the Self will be experienced or seen more in terms of qualities expressed on the finer dimensional levels of reality. As the journey continues, the so-called Ultimate Reality of Brahman will dawn. Living life in the wholeness of existence from a surreal platform that nothing ever happened, nothing will ever happen, and what appears to be happening is nothing. The Brahman realization with only an intellectual understanding, and not the full knowing of Brahman as Self, as a living reality, has caused some spiritual Nondual aspirants to become nihilistic in their worldview. Their interpretation is based solely on conceptualizing Brahman, which only leads to a retardation of spiritual expansion.

On the contrary, the nothingness that is realized and lived is a truth revealing the most delicate inner dimensions of reality. Life goes on as before, but with a more holistic perspective. This realization is from the Source, the Oneness of everything. Just as in Unity Consciousness, everything was experienced as Self, motivated by Self, and emerging from Self Consciousness. In Brahman, the perspective is everything is diminishing in that Void, that nothingness; a kind of reverse perspective that enables the clarity of Brahman to be at ease with the perception that everything emergent is a "no-thing."

> You are an incredible mystery that you will never figure out. To be this mystery consciously is the greatest joy.   —Adyashanti

In the early stages of Consciousness, the motivating energy for the evolutionary shifts in the perspective of consciousness are qualities of Love-Bliss recognized by any culture in human history as godliness. We have seen clearly on a mundane level what energy pulls and draws people together as a nation, society, and family. It is the principle of solidarity in Unity. The Heart center's fourth chakra generates that unifying feeling or emotion that quickly transcends separation. It is also curiously centered in the middle of the seven primary chakras. The Heart unites the primal three lower chakras with the Divine higher three chakras with God's Love and Grace. This unification is initially experienced when Unity Consciousness dawns and everything is perceived as the Self. More so, the Love-Bliss associated with this recognition reverberates through the strata of manifestation. The laws of nature are becoming awake as well. It is also worth mentioning that in Vedic Tradition, the laws of nature are called "Devata." These are the energies from the celestial level of creation that structure and maintain physical life. The terminology in phonetics between the Latin word Divina, and the Sanskrit, Devata for the glory of Divinity, is so similar in sound appreciation that it is worth mentioning the parallels from a historical perspective.

David Buckland, a Vedic scholar who has a master's degree in Maharishi Vedic Science, explains that the development of consciousness from the initial realization of Self in Cosmic Consciousness to Unity Consciousness resembles what is occurring during the onset of the Brahman stage. The similarity rests in any conscious realities expressed during the progression of expanding consciousness is ultimately stripped away. Dualistic ignorance is uncovered in the initial awakening to Self. The "Consciousness is all there is" paradigm, recognized in the Unity stage, is when the illusion of material appearance is transcended. Everything is seen as the one vast ocean of Consciousness. Finally, the apparent development and blossoming of Consciousness Dynamics within Brahman is also transcended, going beyond the depth of Self. A clearing out of **Is-ness**, consciousness being Self and perceived as Self in expression. And from that nothingness, a space appears to be known. This progressive taking away or shedding of reality that once seemed and felt authentic underlies the Self coming to know itself fully.

David states in his beautifully all-encompassing and descriptive book, *Our Natural Potential* when referring to the movement within Brahman to Para-Brahman:

> In Brahman, we discover the origin of consciousness. We can say there are two aspects or meta-qualities: alertness and liveliness. Alertness is what allows Brahman to know itself. Liveliness is what motivates that. Liveliness stirs alertness to become aware. More liveliness and alertness flows, curves back on itself, and becomes self-aware. This is the origin of the dynamics of consciousness, but from a Brahman perspective, this simply supports an appearance. It doesn't arise as something distinct or actually creates something.
>
> —pp. 129, *Our Natural Potential*, David Buckland

When alertness and liveliness flow, it is the quality of Divine love from that very refined, very subtle level of that impulse of love. Intention propels liveliness and alertness, enabling awareness to look back on itself and develop the perspective of a more profound value, Para-Brahman or pure Divinity.

David goes on to illuminate the subtleties of this expansion of awareness as Para-Brahman:

> This is far beyond belief. Even the mechanism of experience in consciousness has been transcended. Yet it is still something we can live. We can say Divinity is Omnipresent, it is everything. But it is not the appearance of the world alone. It is what is behind that, the profound intelligence and energy that supports the world's appearance. Omniscient is also used to describe Divinity. It is profoundly

self-knowing, supporting all the flow of energy and laws of nature that sustain the careful balance of the world. Divinity is said to be Omnipotent. All the energy in the universe is a tiny reflection of the potency of Divinity. It is the ultimate causality, the first and final cause. Love in its pure form is the flow of Divinity.

—pp. 139 *Our Natural Potential,* David Buckland

David, in his book, points out the structure of Divinity where there are the seven qualities of the Divine: Being, Action, Power, Love, Intention, Liveliness, and Intelligence. The fourth and middle position is where Divine Love and the flow of love reside. It is that "flow" as seen from the emergence of life from the "Big Bang," nothing other than that, the initial intent of Source curving back on itself to repeatedly know itself as Divine. In that recognition, the knowing of Divinity, not semblance, but the unformed power of Divine nature, reside the origin of consciousness.

That flow or quality of love remains within the essence of self-aware consciousness as the **"I"** hidden deep within Brahman, the afterglow of Divinity. In his lectures, David Buckland writes: "Conscious awareness in nothingness, Brahman, reveals itself as Divinity unseen through the nothingness of appearance. The appearance of conscious awareness is traced back to the Source value as the power behind the appearance. In this process, more and more, the radiance of Divinity is seen as all that there is."

> Penetrate into the center of nothingness. Creep as far as you can into the truth of your nothingness, and then nothingness will disquiet you.
>
> —Miguel de Molinas

In Para-Brahman, the cognition or knowing all seven qualities of Divinity are revealed in their splendor. The **"I"** where the perspective is nothingness is known in its Totality as Divinity. Totality, even from a perceptual seeing, occurs where all fields of awareness, primary, secondary, tertiary, and so on, are perceived as one seamless seeing. The seeing or knowing of Divinity in all things, yet life continues as it does. Life is recognized as a quality in living life, not a stage within the content. It's all a flow of Divinity in diversified energy signatures.

> To know that the Self is context and that, in contrast, the self is content is already a huge leap forward. The naïve seeker merely keeps reshuffling the content. The Source of all that exists is Divinity; thus, all that exists is already perfect. Without that perfection. Nothing could exist. From the viewpoint of enlightenment, one might say that the linear is observed from the context of the nonlinear. To put it differently, existence is the manifestation of Divinity as form. In and of itself, the Universe.
>
> —David Hawkins

Along with David Buckland's acute insights into reality and his intellectual understanding and ability to write clearly and descriptively, one must remember that the moment a word is uttered, or a letter is scribed, a definition as such places a boundary on true values of reality. While dealing primarily with Nondual teachings to encourage lifting the veil of separation, any book falls short in the goal of justifying explanation as truth. Knowledge, handed down verbally or written, has some value and worth, pointing to a higher reality. It offers the recipient moments to acknowledge some aspect within themselves that resonates with the teaching.

Lorn and Lucia Hoff are spiritual teachers from the Vedic Lineage who have developed their style of teachings over the years. Their depth of knowledge and personal experience is unfathomable, and to sit with them in one of their Satsang is a high energy charge in awareness and physiology. They collaborated in a book entitled *The*

Incredible Reality of You. Here are some excerpts from the chapters on Divinity.

> Consciousness is consciousness due to the subtle impulse inherent in pure Nothingness to know and to Be. That stimulus is pure Divinity, the ultimate power source and force creating Consciousness and the universal Intelligence that appears as all existence in the first place. It is the true cause of all causes and the supreme source of the source. There is no distinction between Nothingness and its Supreme Divine power, just as there is no distinction between God and the will of God. It is one thing. Yet, without that primal pure intention of Divine Will, there would be no Consciousness and no Cosmic Intelligence to create and uphold the appearance of creation, and even Nothingness could not be. The Infinite Silence of pure Nothingness is due to the Infinite Dynamism of pure Divinity. They have always been one wholeness.
> —pp. 229 *The Incredible Reality of You,* Lucia and
> Lorn Hoff

This section on Divinity provides a beautiful vision of inherent potential and possibilities that await every human being in their evolutionary journey in the expansion of Self-awareness, Consciousness. It's not a myth gleaned from ancient text, although mythological stories have their value inspirationally. The teachings of Advaita are not some fanciful flights of mood to set one on an only path to freedom. It is reliable knowledge and corroborated by current scientific theory to a high degree. It is the experience of many on Earth now who are going through a transformative change in conscious awareness. Granted, these stages of Brahman and Divinity may seem abstract to the human mind. Even those enjoying the love and bliss of Unity Consciousness have no way of knowing what lies ahead.

> No one can pass the gateless gate. No one's mind
> has ever figured out how and none ever will. No one
> can pass the gateless gate, so be no one.
> —Daniel Schmidt

The writing of this book honors Adi Shankara and his teachings of Advaita/Vedanta, Nondual Realization, and places in perspective the relevance of those teachings in light of Maharishi's Vedic Science the heritage of Indian philosophy and knowledge. It also draws parallels from modern scientific research in physics to quell some skepticism. From such a comparative platform of analysis, the interpretations of current Advaita teaching can be seen as a profound way to move forward to Self-actualize, to see beyond the veil of illusion. Nonduality teachings take one on a spiritual quest to Self-realization. From initial Cosmic reality to Brahman, as the Ultimate Reality, resting as Source energy. And in that Self-realization, "Nothingness" is the value from which all appearance is known and appreciated. From the apparent void, the fullness of Brahman, all is known as Divinity, the power behind Maya. In a Divine display, the illusion is the formation of the manifested universe.

> The correct understanding will be when you realize
> that whatever you have understood so far is invalid.
> —Nisargadatta Maharaj

It's all well and fine to attempt to define Brahman and Divinity, but what does the knowledge of these intricate dynamics of reality eschew for the everyday person in any current life situation? Life is for the living of it. That is where the juice is. The flow of life energy is so simple if it comes from the Heart, ever reaching for more joy and satisfaction, and how about just peace of mind? One will find and do well if the heart perspective is incorporated into daily activity. It's the kindness within shown without that leads not only to the peace of mind but to an ever-increasing natural impulse to explore and expand consciousness. It is a common saying that "It is what it is." Fair enough, accepting life as it unfolds is part of the flow; we won't change by intellectualizing. But at times, overstating "it is what it is" from a shallow perspective is a cop-out and may lead to a resigned attitude towards life. Any change will ultimately come from within, from the profound realization in each of us that love is our core reality and love is a unifying power; it unites in the existence of Oneness.

> All you need is love, love
> Love is all you need.
> John Lennon/Paul McCartney, 1967

> Approach everything every day with love, kindness, and understanding. Open your heart to the unknown, the mystery that is life.
> —Shivada Amrita

BIBLIOGRAPHY

Adyashanti. (2009) The End of Your World: Uncensored Straight Talk on the Nature of Enlightenment. Boulder CO 80306 Sounds True

Adyashanti. (2021) The Direct Way: Thirty Practices to Evoke Awakening. Boulder CO 80306 Sounds True.

Christopher Isherwood. (1971) The Crest Jewel of Discrimination. Viveka-Chudamani. Hollywood, CA 90068 Vedanta Press

David Carse. (2006) Perfect Brilliant Stillness: Beyond the Individual Self. Shelburne, VT 05482 Paragate Publishing.

David "Davidya" Buckland. (2017) Our natural Potential, Beyond Personal Development-The Stages of Enlightenment Courtney BC V9N3W5 Davidya Publishing

David Hawkins. (2013) Power Vs. Force: An Anatomy of Consciousness. Carlsbad, CA 92018 Hay House, Inc.

Deepack Chopra. (2010) The Shadow Effect: Illuminating the Hidden Power of Your True Self. New York NY 10022 Harper Collins, Inc.

Fred Davis. (2013) The Book of Unknowing: From Enlightenment to Embodiment. Columbia, SC 29229 Awakening Clarity Press

Gregg Braden. (2012) The Spontaneous Healing of Belief: Shattering the Paradigm of False Limits. Taos NM, 87571 Hay House, Inc.

Lorn and Lucia Hoff. (2019) The Incredible Reality of You, A Spiritual Guide to the Awakening of Consciousness. Chemainus BC V0R1K0 Awakening World Publishing

Maharishi Mahesh Yogi. (1967/1990) On the Bhagavad-Gita: A New Translation and Commentary. London UK SRM Publications/ Penguin Books/Arkana

Paul Levy. (2018) The Quantum Revelation: A Radical Synthesis of Science and Spirituality. New York NY 10003 Select Books, Inc.

Ric Weinman. (2013) Awakening through the Veils: A Seeker's Guide. Bloomington, IN 47403 Balboa Press

Robert M. Oates, Jr. (2019) Consciousness and the Quantum: The Next Paradigm. Fairfield, IA 52557 MIU Press

ACKNOWLEDGEMENTS

To Roberta Lynn Forem, her long history of spiritual expertise and literary editing made this book shine. I am so grateful for her contribution and the chance to connect.

To David (Davidya) Buckland for his technical information in formulating a book, adding philosophical nuance to areas in my project, and taking time during his busy personal life to write a foreward to this book.

To Kathy McClement, a dear spiritual friend, for her inspiration from the very start of this journey and her beautiful insights before publication.

ABOUT THE AUTHOR

Henry Ulaszonek was initiated into Transcendental Meditation in the autumn of 1970, immediately confirming without question a conscious reality far greater than the identification of a personal me. Could this be possible, and was it akin to some of the incredible experiences of altered reality as a kid? Within a few short years of regular meditation and attending weekend retreats, I found myself in a curious position. A barrage of eyes closed blissful mystical experiences where the Holy Tradition of Masters, and Maharishi Mahesh Yogi often visited me. I decided to drop university studies to become a TM teacher in 1973.

In 1976, special courses for TM teachers called the Age of Enlightenment Governors Training were instructed in the TM-Sidhi program. Techniques parallel to the Yoga Sutras of Patanjali. I recognized during the course what Maharishi meant by integration and wholeness of consciousness. It was also the first time I had abiding experiences of Unity Consciousness.

Soon after, in 1977, while teaching TM and involved with other projects for the TM organization, I met the love of my life and was married with children in no time. I became a householder and decided to build a secure family and career.

In 2010 my kids are now grown, in university or professional life; my wife and I are no longer together. I attended Maharishi International University for a year and participated in the Invincible America program. At that time, I also enrolled in a follow-up course to re-certify my status as a TM instructor. During this entire year of long daily meditation practice, heightened spiritual experiences occupied my conscious reality again.

Sometime later, around 2016, I joined a group of meditators, mainly with a TM background involved with regular meditation retreats on Vancouver Island. This is where I met Lorn and Lucia Hoff. They were spiritually guiding this group with a fascinating twist on the philosophy of enlightenment, something similar to TM but at the same time fresh, new, and inviting. It wasn't long after, through a simple conversation with Lorn and Lucia, what was revealed was something I recognized all along: an always present cosmic reality that the little ego me was interfering with all this time. Soon after, in 2019, while driving back to Vancouver from a retreat session on the island, Unity Consciousness was spontaneously revealed. This abiding level of consciousness, coupled with the group meditation practice of advanced techniques in further refining the depths of consciousness, has prompted me through this journey to acquire the spiritual name Shivada.

Website: advaitaspeaks.com

Printed in the United States
by Baker & Taylor Publisher Services